HOW TO PASS ✓

STANDARD GRADE
ADMINISTRATION

IAN ORD

HODDER
GIBSON
PART OF HACHETTE LIVRE UK

The Publishers would like to thank the following for permission to reproduce copyright material:

Photo credits

Page 102 screengrab reproduced with kind permission of John Lewis plc.

Acknowledgements

Every effort has been made to trace all copyright holders, but if any have been inadvertently overlooked the Publishers will be pleased to make the necessary arrangements at the first opportunity.

Although every effort has been made to ensure that website addresses are correct at time of going to press, Hodder Gibson cannot be held responsible for the content of any website mentioned in this book. It is sometimes possible to find a relocated web page by typing in the address of the home page for a website in the URL window of your browser.

Hachette's policy is to use papers that are natural, renewable and recyclable products and made from wood grown in sustainable forests. The logging and manufacturing processes are expected to conform to the environmental regulations of the country of origin.

Orders: please contact Bookpoint Ltd, 130 Milton Park, Abingdon, Oxon OX14 4SB. Telephone: (44) 01235 827720. Fax: (44) 01235 400454. Lines are open 9.00 – 5.00, Monday to Saturday, with a 24-hour message answering service. Visit our website at www.hoddereducation.co.uk. Hodder Gibson can be contacted direct on: Tel: 0141 848 1609; Fax: 0141 889 6315; email: hoddergibson@hodder.co.uk

© Ian Ord 2008

First published in 2008 by

Hodder Gibson, an imprint of Hodder Education,

An Hachette Livre UK Company,

2a Christie Street

Paisley PA1 1NB

Impression number	5 4 3 2 1
Year	2012 2011 2010 2009 2008

Cover photo © Rob Wilkinson/Alamy

Illustrations by Tony Wilkins Design

Typeset in 10.5 on 14pt Frutiger Light by Phoenix Photosetting, Chatham, Kent

Printed in Great Britain by Martins The Printers, Berwick-upon-Tweed

A catalogue record for this title is available from the British Library

ISBN-13: 978 0340 957 677

CONTENTS

INTRODUCTION

Standard Grade Administration is a course which seeks to give pupils a real-life insight into the administrative duties and tasks undertaken within a modern organisation. To achieve this, the course covers two main Areas of Study. These are:

1   Administrative Support

2   Information and Communications Technology (ICT).

Within each Area of Study the following topics are covered:

Area of Study 1

◆ Introduction to Business Organisations
◆ The Working Environment
◆ Storage and Retrieval of Information
◆ Reprographics
◆ Sources of Information
◆ Preparation and Presentation of Information
◆ Travel.

Area of Study 2

◆ Communications
◆ Databases
◆ File Management
◆ Spreadsheets
◆ Word Processing.

Course Assessment

The Scottish Qualifications Authority (SQA) is responsible for assessing all candidates who complete the Standard Grade Administration course. It assesses each candidate against three criteria, called assessable elements. These are:

◆ Knowledge and Understanding (KU)
◆ Problem Solving (PS)
◆ Practical Abilities (PA).

Every candidate is awarded a grade for each element which is displayed on their SQA Certificate. The KU and PS grades are based on a candidate's performance in the SQA's Standard Grade Administration examination. The PA grade is based on their performance in the SQA's Standard Grade Administration Practical Abilities Project. The grades that can be achieved for each element are as follows:

Credit Level	General Level	Foundation Level	No Award
Grade 1	Grade 3	Grade 5	Grade 7
Grade 2	Grade 4	Grade 6	

Standard Grade Administration Examination

This is a written exam which is externally set and marked by the SQA. The exam covers the whole course and all questions are either KU or PS. As with other Standard Grades, there are three papers: Credit, General and Foundation. Each candidate sits two papers, either Credit and General or General and Foundation. As each candidate sits two papers, only their best grade in each element (KU and PS) is shown on their SQA certificate.

Standard Grade Administration Practical Abilities Project

The Practical Abilities project involves completing a number of integrated ICT tasks using a computer. As with the written exam, it is externally set and marked by the SQA. Although set at three levels, each candidate undertakes only one project, at Credit, General or Foundation level. The grade achieved in the Practical Abilities project is shown on a candidate's SQA certificate.

The Overall Award for Standard Grade Administration

A candidate's overall award for the course is calculated by applying the following weightings to each element:

◆ Knowledge and Understanding 30%
◆ Problem Solving 30%
◆ Practical Abilities 40%.

The Course Notes

The course notes have been written to assist with each part of the course. The first seven chapters concentrate on the written examination which assess KU and PS. At the end of each of these chapters a range of exam-style questions have been set. Chapter 8 focuses on the Practical Abilities project.

Although the first seven chapters use the same section headings as those of Area Study 1, it is important to note that relevant material from Area of Study 2 has been added at appropriate points.

INTRODUCTION TO BUSINESS ORGANISATIONS: ORGANISATION OF DEPARTMENTS

Organisation Charts

Trying to describe how an organisation has been set up using words alone is far too complicated. This is why many organisations create an organisation chart.

As can be seen from Abacus Enterprise's organisation chart on the next page, an organisation chart is a diagram which shows:

◆ The management structure of an organisation.

◆ How big the organisation is.

◆ What departments are in an organisation. For example, in Abacus Enterprises there are Purchases, Sales and Marketing, Human Resources, Finance and Administration Departments.

◆ In which departments certain people work. For example, Mrs Patak works in the Sales and Marketing Department.

◆ What each person's job title is. For example, Mr Jarvis is the Finance Director.

◆ Who is in charge of whom. For example, Miss Clarke is in charge of Miss Popal and Miss Popal is in charge of Mr Younis.

◆ How many people work directly for each person. For example, seven Operations Assistants work for Mr Dent.

◆ How information should pass through the organisation.

The Benefits of using an Organisation Chart

The benefits of using an organisation chart can be divided into three areas. These are:

Employees
An employee benefits from an organisation chart as it shows: i) where they 'fit into' the organisation, ii) who their manager is, iii) who they are in charge of, iv) what department they work in and who else works there, v) how information is passed through the organisation, and vi) how big the organisation is by looking at how many departments and people are on the chart.

Visitors
A visitor benefits from an organisation chart as it shows: i) which person should be contacted in the organisation to answer a particular query, ii) which department the person being visited works in, iii) who is in charge of whom, iv) what different

Organisation Chart

ABACUS
ENTERPRISES

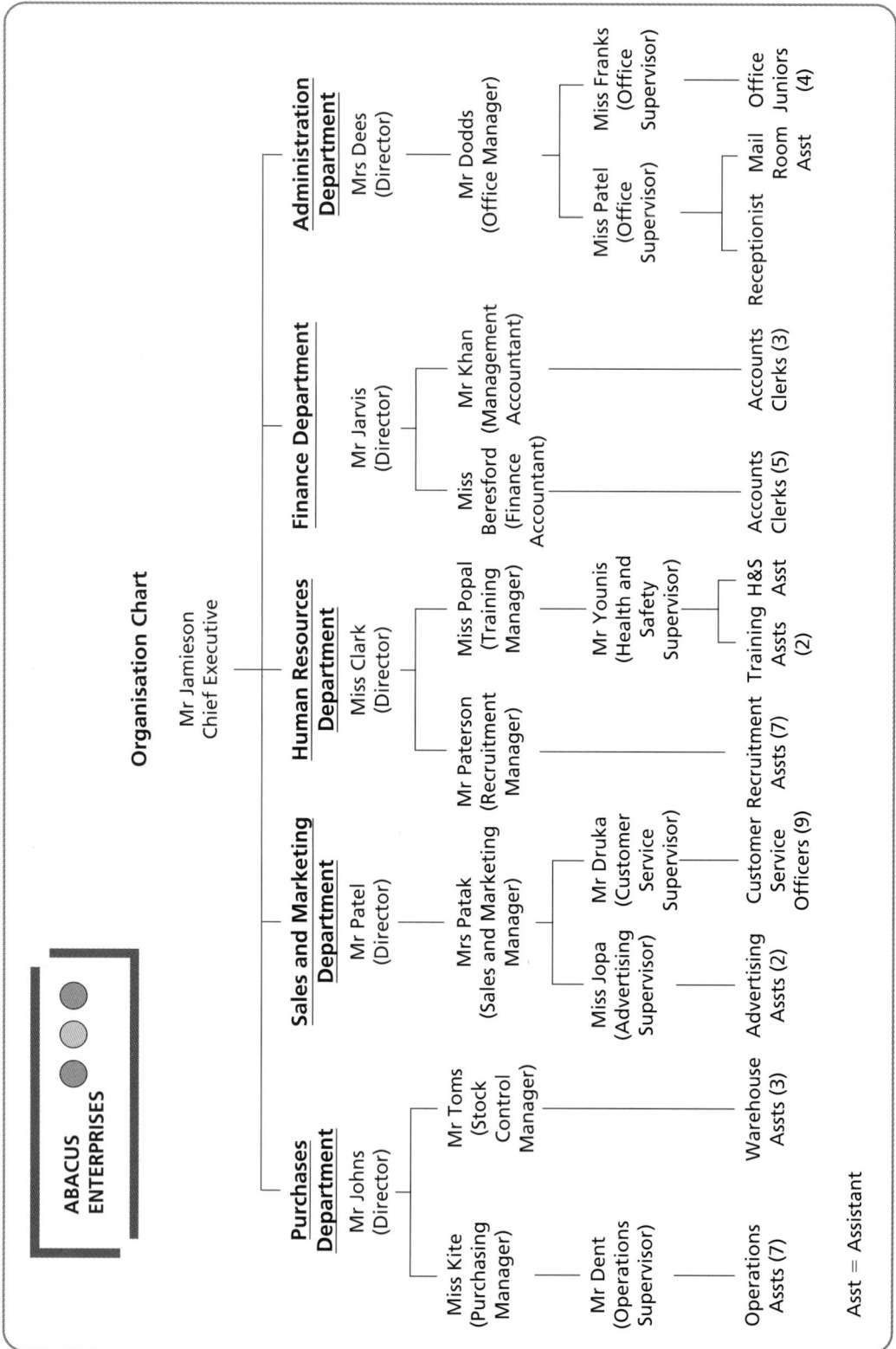

Figure 1.1 Organisation chart

departments are in the organisation and what the organisation does, and v) how big the organisation is by looking at how many departments and people are on the chart.

Restructuring

The benefits of using an organisation chart after an organisation restructures are: i) it will be easier for employees to understand how the organisation's management structure has changed, ii) employees will find it easier to work out if the department they work in has changed. For example, has it got bigger or smaller?, iii) employees will find it easier to work out how they now 'fit into' the organisation. For example, is the employee now in a more senior position?, and iv) it will be easier to work out if there have been any changes in the management team.

The Drawbacks of using an Organisation Chart

Although using an organisation chart can be useful, there are a number of drawbacks:

◆ The organisation chart can become dated very quickly. If employees leave and new ones join, the organisation chart will have to be updated.

◆ An organisation chart can be difficult to understand if it contains too much information.

◆ After restructuring, an organisation chart will display the wrong information unless it is updated.

◆ An organisation chart is usually not big enough to show everybody that works in an organisation.

Describing what an Organisation Chart Shows

When describing what an organisation chart shows, it is important to use certain key terms.

Hints and Tips

Make sure you know all the organisation chart key terms. Pupils often provide poor definitions to such questions in the written examination.

Span of Control

This describes how many people a manager directly supervises or is directly responsible for. For example, Mr Jarvis has two people working for him (see right). This means that his span of control is two. As he only has two people working for him it can be said that he has a narrow span of control. However, if he were supervising a lot of people it would be said that he had a wide span of control.

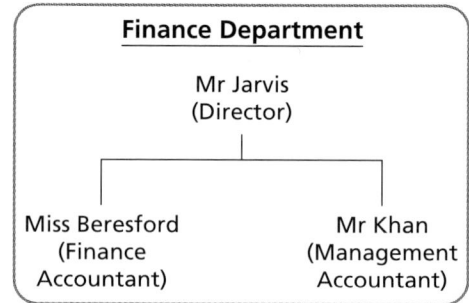

```
              Finance Department

                 Mr Jarvis
                 (Director)
           ┌─────────────┴─────────────┐
     Miss Beresford                 Mr Khan
       (Finance                   (Management
      Accountant)                 Accountant)
```

Figure 1.2 Span of control

Lateral Relationship

This describes the relationship that employees who are at the same level and within the same department have. In the diagram above, Miss Beresford and Mr Khan work for Mr Jarvis in the Finance Department. This means they have a lateral relationship.

Chain of Command

This shows who is in charge of whom and therefore how instructions are passed down an organisation. For example, Miss Clarke is in charge of Miss Popal, and Miss Popal is in charge of Mr Younis (see below).

In a chain command, the higher an employee is, the greater their level of responsibility and the greater their level of authority.

Superior and Subordinate

These are the words used to describe the relationship between employees at different levels on an organisation chart. The employee who is at the higher level is called the superior, while the employee below them is called the subordinate. For example, in the diagram at right, Miss Clark is superior to Miss Popal; and Mr Younis is subordinate to Miss Popal.

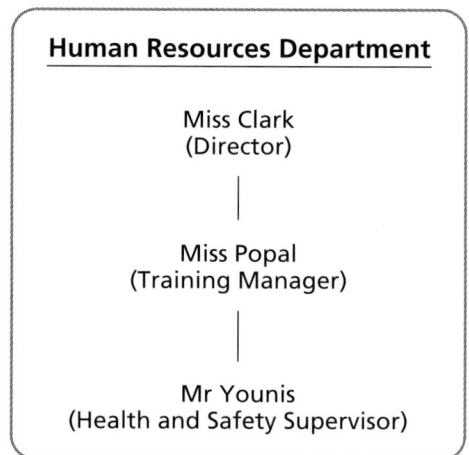

```
        Human Resources Department

                 Miss Clark
                 (Director)
                     │
                 Miss Popal
              (Training Manager)
                     │
                 Mr Younis
         (Health and Safety Supervisor)
```

Figure 1.3 Chain of command

Line Relationship

In the chain of command shown above, you can see that each person in the chain has been joined by a direct line. This vertical line is what is called a line relationship. A line relationship therefore describes the direct link between a superior and the subordinate that works for them. It also shows who has authority over whom and how instructions are passed between manager and employee.

Authority

This refers to how much power an employee has. For example, in the chain of command on the previous page, Miss Clark, the Human Resources Director, has the authority to tell Miss Popal, the Training Manager, what to do. Furthermore, as Miss Clark is in charge of the Human Resources Department she has a lot of authority.

Level of Responsibility

This refers to an employee's position within an organisation. The further up the chain of command an employee is, the greater their level of responsibility. For example, Miss Clark has a greater level of responsibility than Mr Younis.

Delegation

This describes the process in which a manager/superior gives one of their employees/subordinates a task to do that he would normally carry out himself. For example, Miss Clark could delegate a task to Miss Popal.

Accountability

An employee is said to have accountability when the completion of a task is their responsibility. If the task is not completed, the employee will be accountable for failing to do so. Should this happen, the employee will be expected to explain why the task was not completed.

Organisation Charts and Pyramid Structures

Another way to look at an organisation chart is through a pyramid structure. As the diagram below shows, the pyramid shape is a lot less complicated and shows the different levels of management in the organisation. For example, at the bottom of the structure are the employees and at the top is the Chief Executive. It is also interesting to note that as you move up the pyramid there are less and less people at each level. As you would expect, people at the same level on the pyramid have the same level of authority and responsibility.

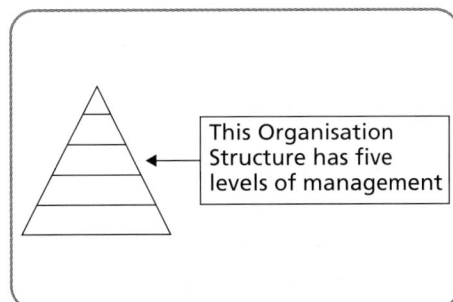

This Organisation Structure has five levels of management

Figure 1.4 Pyramid Structure

Two Different Shapes

There are two main pyramid shapes which show the management structure of an organisation. The first is a flat management structure and the second is a tall management structure.

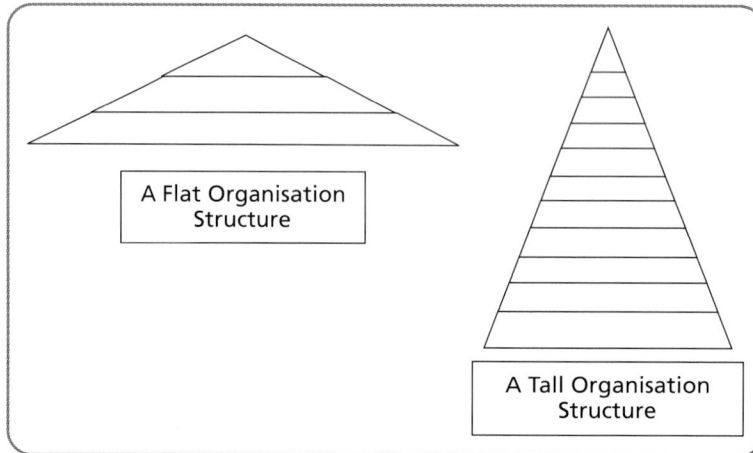

A Flat Organisation Structure

A Tall Organisation Structure

Figure 1.5 Two pyramid structures

As you can see the two structures are quite different. The flat structure only has a few levels of management, meaning it has a short chain of command, whereas the tall structure has many levels of management, and therefore has a long chain of command. Furthermore, in a flat structure a manager can expect to be supervising quite a few employees, which means they will have a wide span of control. On the other hand, in a tall structure, a manager will be supervising only a few people, so they will have a narrow span of control.

Flat Management Structure

Advantages: i) as there are not many levels of management, information will move quickly through the organisation, ii) decisions should be implemented quickly as the chain of command is shorter, iii) employees at the bottom of the structure are given responsibility and are allowed to make decisions which should motivate them, and iv) such organisations tend to be friendlier as everyone in the organisation knows everyone else.

Disadvantages: i) a manager usually has to supervise a lot of people because their span of control is wide. This can be difficult and stressful, ii) there are few opportunities for promotion because there are not many levels of management, and iii) employees will need training in order to take on their added responsibilities.

Tall Management Structure

Advantages: i) managers tend to have narrow spans of control which makes it easy to supervise staff, ii) as there are many levels of management there are promotion opportunities, and iii) employees are given very specific jobs which they can become very efficient at doing.

Disadvantages: i) employees can become bored and de-motivated because their jobs are too simple and boring, and because they are not given any responsibility; ii) information and decisions take a long time to move through the organisation as there are so many levels of management; and iii) such organisations tend to be unfriendly because people at the top do not know the people at the bottom.

Changes in Organisation Structure

An organisation's structure can change in many ways. The main ways that this can happen are explained below:

Growth

This occurs when the organisation has been successful and decides to expand. The organisation will employ more people, produce more products and may move to larger premises.

By growing in size, the organisation's structure should increase in size and more levels of management or new departments are added. In the diagram at right, two new levels of management have been added

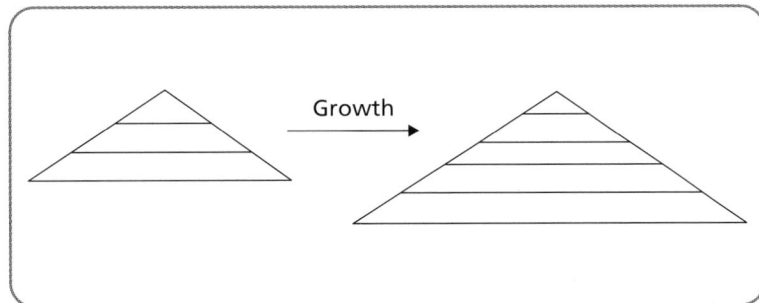

Figure 1.6 Growth (new levels of management added)

Downsizing

Downsizing occurs when an organisation becomes smaller in size. Staff are made redundant in order to reduce costs and make the organisation more efficient. Those employees who remain will be expected to take on more responsibility.

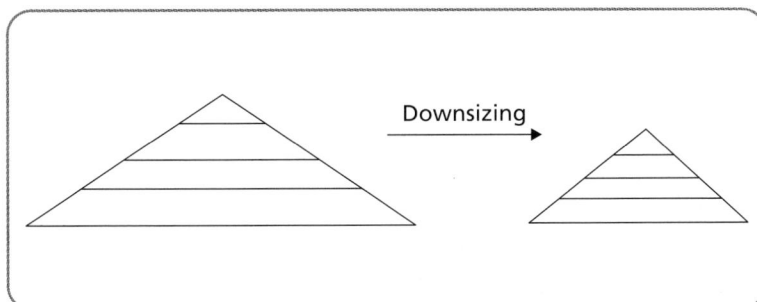

Figure 1.7 Downsizing

HOW TO PASS STANDARD GRADE ADMINISTRATION

The decision to downsize may be taken because:

◆ **The organisation is not doing very well:** Employees will be made redundant and the organisation's level of production will fall.

◆ **New technology is being introduced:** New technology, such as e-commerce or new production machines, is introduced to replace employees and cut costs. The organisation should become more efficient and the level of production may actually increase.

◆ **Merger of two departments:** Two departments, for example Finance and Administration, are joined together. Some employees that did similar work in each of the separate departments will be made redundant. For example, only one director will be required to run the larger department.

◆ **Management Structure simplified:** Layers of management are removed from the organisation. All employees that were in those layers are made redundant. See de-layering below for more detail.

◆ **Department closed down:** A department or section, such as IT support, is closed down. All the employees in that department are made redundant. Should the organisation require IT support in the future they buy it in from another organisation. See outsourcing below for more detail.

De-layering

This occurs because the organisation thinks its current organisation structure does not work very well. The organisation will remove layers of management, meaning it moves from a tall structure to a flatter structure. The

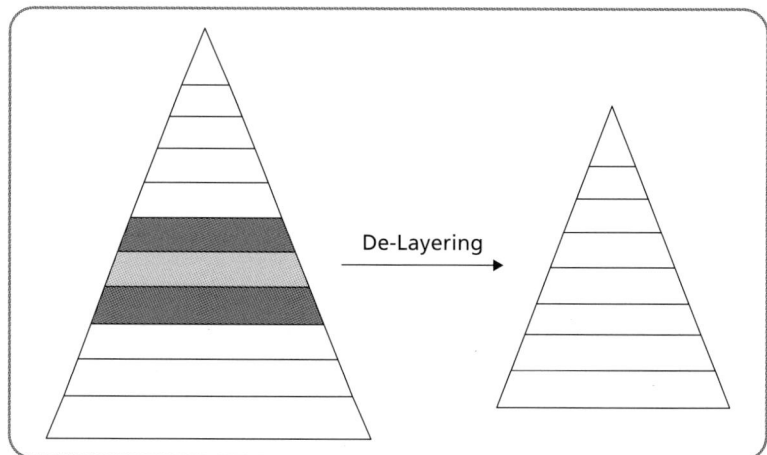

Figure 1.8 Delayering

effect of this is that many employees will lose their jobs and remaining workers will be expected to take on more responsibility. However, as the structure is flatter, information should flow more easily and decisions should be made more quickly within the organisation.

Outsourcing

This occurs because the organisation wants to concentrate on its core activities. Instead of undertaking certain activities, an organisation buys in the service from another business. For example, instead of creating their own advertising campaigns, an organisation may ask a specialist advertising firm to do so. The effect of outsourcing is to downsize the organisation.

By using a specialist firm, the organisation is likely to benefit from a better service that is more cost effective. The organisation structure should also be easier to manage as it will have been simplified. All those staff who were part of the organisation's advertising team will be made redundant.

Centralisation of Departmental Function

This occurs when certain activities that are undertaken in all departments are centralised in one department. For example, the administrative function may be centralised by moving all the administration assistants for each separate department to a centralised Administration department.

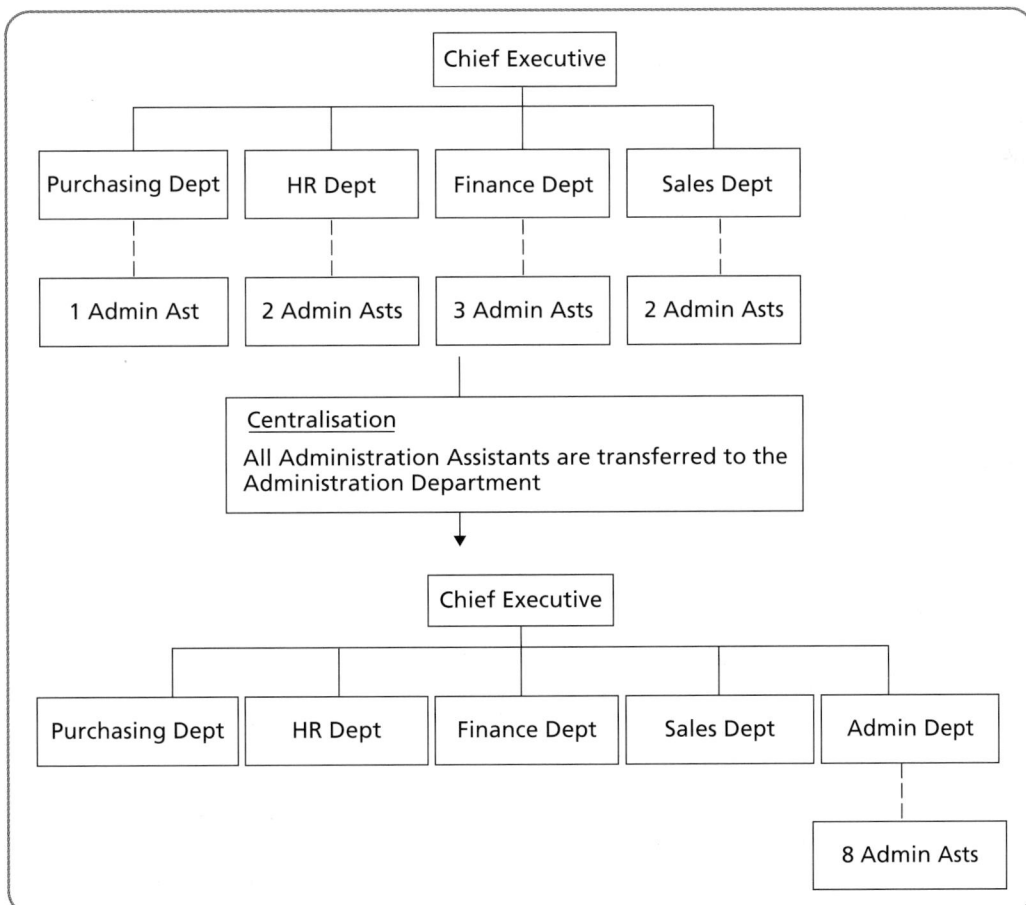

Figure 1.9 Centralisation of Administrative Function

Decentralisation of Departmental Function

This occurs when the activities of one department are assigned to other departments. For example, the administration department may be closed and the administration staff within it assigned to other departments in the organisation.

Questions

1 Explain one benefit to an employee and one benefit to a visitor of making an organisation chart. (2 KU – G)

2 Explain what is meant by the following terms:

- Chain of Command
- Level of Responsibility
- Lateral Relationship. (3 KU – G)

3 Describe two advantages of a flat organisational structure. (2 KU – G)

4 Teeside plc is an electronics firm located in Dundee. The following problems have been identified with their organisation:

- Information takes too long to pass between the different levels of management.
- Staff are bored because of the repetitive nature of their jobs.

Recommend a way in which Teeside plc could be re-organised to solve these problems. Justify your answer. (2 PS – C)

5 Explain two effects restructuring may have on an organisation. (2 KU – C)

INTRODUCTION TO BUSINESS ORGANISATIONS: KEY FUNCTIONS OF DEPARTMENTS

Departments in an Organisation

Most organisations are usually divided up into departments, called functional areas. The main functional areas or departments you will come across are:

◆ Purchasing Department

◆ Sales and Marketing Department

◆ Human Resources Department

◆ Finance Department

◆ Computing Services Department

◆ Administration Department.

Purchasing Department

The Purchasing Department's main role is purchasing and storing stock for the organisation. When it does this, it should be looking for the best quality stock at the lowest price. Specific duties undertaken by the Purchases Department include: i) storing the stock in a warehouse when it arrives, ii) checking the stock that has been received against the delivery note, iii) keeping stock records so it knows how much it has, iv) preparing purchase orders for new stock, and v) asking possible new suppliers for quotes, catalogues and price lists.

Specific jobs undertaken within the Purchases Department include:

Purchasing Manager
A Purchasing Manager will be involved in: i) managing the Purchases Department budget, ii) interviewing staff for the department, iii) negotiating with suppliers over prices, and iv) setting targets for departmental and individual performance.

Buyer
A Buyer will be involved in: i) negotiating with suppliers over prices, ii) researching the internet and supplier catalogues for best prices, iii) visiting suppliers, and iv) attending supplier exhibitions.

Stock Controller
A Stock Controller will be involved in: i) maintaining stock records, ii) making sure stock is kept safely and securely, iii) making sure stock is used in the correct order i.e. oldest first, and iv) making sure out-of-date stock is disposed of.

Warehouse Supervisor

A Warehouse Supervisor will be involved in: i) making sure health and safety policy is followed in the warehouse, ii) making sure all staff in the warehouse carry out their duties, and iii) checking all deliveries against delivery notes.

Purchases Department Administration Assistant

A Purchases Department Administration Assistant will be involved in: i) completing purchase orders, ii) contacting suppliers to request a catalogue of prices, iii) filing supplier catalogues, and iv) maintaining a database of all suppliers' names and addresses.

Documents and forms used within the Purchasing Department include:

Purchase Order Form: This form is completed when the organisation wants to place an order with another business. On the form, the items and quantity required are listed so that the other business knows what to send.

Delivery Note: This is sent to the organisation with the items that were requested on the purchase order form. The delivery note should be checked against the items received to make sure they are identical.

ICT used to assist the Purchasing Department includes:

◆ A word processing software application could be used to complete a purchase order form.

◆ A spreadsheet software application could be used to calculate how much certain orders will cost or to maintain a record of how many items of stock are held.

◆ A database software application could be used to keep a record of all stock or to maintain a record of all suppliers' details.

◆ An e-mail software application could be used to send purchase orders to suppliers.

◆ The internet could be used to purchase items online or to search for new suppliers.

◆ A fax machine could be used to send purchase orders to suppliers.

◆ A public address system could be used to contact employees who are working in the warehouse.

Sales and Marketing Department

The Sales and Marketing Department's main role is to advertise and sell what the organisation makes. Specific duties undertaken by the Sales and Marketing Department include: i) dealing with customers, ii) undertaking market research and analysing the results, iii) sending out information to customers e.g. catalogues, price lists, iv) making-up adverts, v) dealing with customer complaints, and vi) taking orders from customers.

Specific jobs undertaken within the Sales and Marketing Department include:

Sales Manager
A Sales manager will be involved in: i) motivating sales staff to sell more, ii) setting targets for sales staff, iii) meeting important customers, iv) interviewing staff for the department, and v) negotiating with customers over price.

Advertising Manager
An Advertising Manager will be involved in: i) interviewing staff for the department, ii) coming up with new advertising campaigns, iii) attending trade fairs to promote the organisation's products, and iv) managing the advertising budget.

Market Research Assistant
A Market Research Assistant will be involved in: i) interviewing customers, ii) setting market research questions, and iii) analysing market research results.

Sales Supervisor
A Sales Supervisor will be involved in: i) organising a sales team, ii) motivating a sales team, iii) dealing with customer complaints, and iv) selling products to customers.

Sales and Marketing Administration Assistant
A Sales and Marketing Administration Assistant will be involved in: i) keeping a record of all sales in a spreadsheet, ii) maintaining a database of all customers' details, iii) sending out catalogues and promotional literature to customers, and iv) creating advertising leaflets that will be sent to customers.

Documents and forms used within the Sales and Marketing Department include:

Purchase Order Form: This form should be received from a customer when a sale is made. Once received, the organisation will know what to send out.

ICT used to assist the Sales and Marketing Department includes:

- A word processing software application could be used to prepare letters or price lists to be sent to customers.
- A desk top publishing software application could be used to prepare adverts and catalogues.
- A spreadsheet software application could be used to keep a record of all sales made by employees or to display a chart of sales during a certain period.
- A database software application could be used to maintain a record of customers' details.
- A presentation software application could be used to give a presentation to a customer or at an exhibition.
- An email software application could be used to send information such as a price list to a customer.

◆ The internet could be used to undertake market research or to set up an internet site from which customers can purchase products.

◆ A fax could be used to send a customer a price list.

◆ A pager or mobile phone could be used to contact sales staff whilst out of the office.

Human Resources or Personnel Department

The Human Resources Department's main role is to deal with all issues that relate to the workers or staff in an organisation. Specific duties undertaken by the Human Resources Department include: i) training staff, ii) employing or recruiting new staff, iii) making sure the organisation is aware of laws that affect workers, iv) keeping staff records up to date, v) carry out job interviews, and vi) disciplining staff e.g. giving warnings and firing them.

Specific jobs undertaken within the Human Resources Department include:

Human Resources Manager
A Human Resources Manager will be involved in: i) interviewing staff for the department, ii) motivating staff that work in the department, iii) managing the Human Resources budget, and iv) giving advice to other departments on human resource legislation.

Employee Relations Officer
An Employee Relations Officer will be involved in: i) speaking to staff about any problems or complaints they have, ii) raising any issues or problems staff have with senior management, iii) representing staff at disciplinary hearings, and iv) liaising with Trade Unions on staff issues.

Training Manager
A Training Manager will be involved in: i) Training senior staff, ii) arranging training events, and iii) managing the training budget.

Health and Safety Officer
A Health and Safety Officer will be involved in: i) undertaking health and safety checks throughout the workplace, ii) providing employees with health and safety advice and training, and iii) creating health and safety procedures for the workplace.

Human Resources Administration Assistant
A Human Resources Administration Assistant will be involved in: i) maintaining a database of all employees' details, ii) filing application forms, iii) word processing letters to send to job applicants invited to interview, and iv) sending out application forms.

Documents and forms used within the Human Resources Department include:

Job Description: This document describes the main tasks and duties that will be undertaken in a job. A job description is sent out with all job applications so that applicants know what the job involves.

Person Specification: This document describes the main qualities and characteristics e.g. confidence, ICT skills, needed by an employee to be successful in a job. A person specification can be used to assess all candidates' application forms in order to decide who should be invited to interview.

ICT used to assist the Human Resources Department includes:

◆ A word processing software application could be used to prepare:

◇ A letter to be sent to applicants inviting them to interview.

◇ A list of employees attending a training course.

◇ A health and safety notice.

◆ A spreadsheet software application could be used to manage the Human Resources budget.

◆ A database software application could be used to maintain a record of all employees' details.

◆ A presentation software application could be used to give a presentation to employees on new health and safety procedures.

◆ An email software application could be used to contact applicants for a job interview.

◆ The internet could be used to display job adverts.

◆ The intranet could be used to display internal job adverts or new updated health and safety procedures.

◆ A telephone could be used to contact successful job applicants.

Finance Department

The Finance Department's main role is to deal with all the money that the organisation receives and pays out. Specific duties undertaken by the Finance Department include: i) preparing financial information e.g. trading, profit and loss account, balance sheet, ii) sending out cheques to suppliers after they have received an invoice, iii) preparing and send out invoices, credit notes and statements of account to customers, iv) paying cheques received from customers into the bank, v) calculating wages and paying employees, and vi) calculating how much tax the organisation should pay.

Specific jobs undertaken within the Finance Department include:

Finance Manager

A Finance Manager will be involved in: i) managing the Finance Department's budget, ii) providing advice to other departments on how to manage budgets, iii) interviewing staff for the department, and iv) preparing financial information.

Accountant

An Accountant will be involved in: i) preparing financial statements for senior management, ii) analysing financial information, iii) calculating profits and losses that the organisation makes, and iv) preparing tax returns.

Wages Clerk

A Wages Clerk will be involved in: i) calculating wages, ii) paying wages electronically, iii) counting out money to go into wage packets, and iv) preparing wage slips.

Credit Controller

A Credit Controller will be involved in: i) authorising the payment of suppliers, ii) chasing customers for payment, iii) authorising credit being provided to customers, and iv) declaring some customers' bad debts.

Finance Department Administration Assistant

A Finance Department Administration Assistant will be involved in: i) taking cash and cheques received from customers to the bank, ii) preparing spreadsheets to display financial information, and iii) preparing invoices, credit notes and statements to be sent to customers.

Documents and forms used within the Finance Department include:

Invoice: This is a document that is sent with an order to let a customer know how much they are due the organisation. On the invoice it will state how much is due, VAT and any discount available for prompt payment.

Credit Note: This is a document that is sent to a customer when they return goods to the organisation because they are faulty. On the credit note it will list what goods have been returned, how much they are worth and the reason for their return.

Statement of Account: This is a document which lists all the goods a customer has purchased and returned over a given period of time. It will show any payments made to the account and how much is still outstanding.

ICT used to assist the Finance Department includes:

◆ A word processing software application could be used to prepare invoices, credit notes and statements of account.

◆ A spreadsheet software application could be used to calculate wages and prepare financial information.

◆ A database software application could be used to maintain a record of all customer contact details and credit limits.

◆ A presentation software application could be used to give a presentation to other departments on the financial position of the organisation.

◆ An email software application could be used to contact customers who have not paid their bills.

◆ A fax could be used to send a customer an invoice, credit note or statement of account.

◆ A telephone could be used to contact customers who have not paid their invoices.

Hints and Tips

Make sure you know what tasks Administrative Assistants in each of the functional departments undertake. It is a regular examination question.

Computing Services Department

The Computing Services Department's main function is to deal with all an organisation's ICT (Information Communication and Technology) facilities and requirements. Specific duties undertaken by the Computing Services Department include: i) managing the organisation's computer network, ii) repairing any software, hardware or network faults, iii) testing computer hardware, iv) installing new software and hardware, and v) purchasing new software and hardware.

Specific jobs undertaken within the Computing Services Department include:

Computing Services Manager:
A Computing Services Manager will be involved in: i) interviewing staff for the department, ii) managing the Computing Services budget, and iii) deciding what software and hardware should be purchased.

IT Support Technician:
An IT Support Technician will be involved in: i) repairing any faults with software and hardware, ii) testing new software and hardware before it is installed, and iii) installing new software and hardware.

Programmer:
A Programmer will be involved in: i) creating new software, and ii) writing and designing new software.

Computing Services Administration Assistant:
A Computing Services Administration Assistant will be involved in: i) taking calls from other departments about software and hardware problems, ii) maintaining a

record of all hardware and software owned by the organisation, and iii) marking computer hardware with security marks.

ICT used to assist the Computing Services Department includes:

◆ A word processing software application could be used to prepare an ICT Fault form.

◆ A spreadsheet software application could be used to manage the Computer Service budget.

◆ A database software application could be used to maintain a record of all software and hardware that the organisation owns.

◆ An email software application could be used to provide staff with updates on the repairing of software and hardware.

◆ The internet could be used to search for new software and hardware that the organisation may require.

◆ A pager or a mobile phone could be used to contact IT Support technicians while out on a job.

Administration Department

The administrative function in an organisation can either be centralised or decentralised. If centralised, all administrative tasks such as photocopying, sending mail, arranging travel and filing are undertaken within an Administration Department. However, if the administrative function is decentralised, all administrative tasks are undertaken within each individual department.

The benefits and drawbacks of having a centralised Administration Department are:

Benefits

◆ A more efficient service can be provided by a specialist Administration Department.

◆ Noisy equipment such as photocopiers no longer require to be located in individual departments.

◆ Basic and boring tasks such as filing and franking mail will not be overlooked.

◆ More space will be available in other departments if staff are moved to an Administration Department.

◆ It will be easier and more cost effective to introduce new equipment such as scanners.

Drawbacks

◆ Passing work to and from the Administrative Department may be difficult and time consuming.

◆ Urgent tasks may be delayed if the Administration Department is located some distance away.

- If the communication between the Administration Department and the other departments is poor the quality of work may suffer.

Specific duties undertaken by a centralised Administration Department include:

- Typing up letters and other business documents.
- Dealing with incoming and outgoing mail.
- Keeping filing systems up to date and accurate.
- Dealing with phone calls received by the business.
- Photocopying/reprographics.
- Making travel arrangements.

Specific jobs undertaken within a centralised Administration Department would include:

Office Manager
An Office Manager will be involved in: i) supervising and motivating administration staff, ii) liaising with other departments to find out what work needs to be done, iii) interviewing staff for the department, and iv) checking completed work for quality.

Filing Clerk
A Filing Clerk will be involved in: i) filing customer records, ii) making sure all records are kept neat, tidy and in order, and iii) delivering requested files to members of staff.

Reprographics Assistant
A Reprographics Assistant will be involved in: i) photocopying documents, ii) finishing documents e.g. stapling, punching and binding, and iii) maintaining a record of all copyrighted documents that have been photocopied.

Mailroom Assistant
A Mailroom Assistant will be involved in: i) franking mail, ii) weighing and pricing mail, iii) picking up and delivering mail from departments, and iv) delivering mail to the Post Office.

Specific ways in which functional departments are supported by a centralised Administration Department include:

Purchasing Department: The Administration Department assist by:

- Completing purchase orders and sending them to the suppliers.
- Contacting suppliers to request catalogues.
- Creating and maintaining a database of all suppliers' names and addresses.

Sales and Marketing Department: The Administration Department assist by:

- Creating and maintaining a spreadsheet of all sales figures.
- Creating and maintaining a database of all customers' details.

◆ Sending out catalogues and promotional literature to customers.

◆ Creating advertising leaflets that will be sent to customers.

Human Resources or Personnel Department: The Administration Department assist by:

◆ Creating and maintaining a database of all employees' details.

◆ Filing application forms.

◆ Word processing letters to send to job applicants invited to an interview.

◆ Sending out application forms.

Finance Department: The Administration Department assist by:

◆ Taking cash and cheques received from customers to the bank.

◆ Creating and preparing spreadsheets to display financial information.

◆ Preparing and posting invoices, credit notes and statements of account to be sent to customers.

Computing Services Department: The Administration Department assist by:

◆ Taking calls from other departments about software and hardware problems.

◆ Maintaining a record of all hardware and software owned by the organisation.

◆ Marking computer hardware with security marks.

Questions

1   Suggest and justify two types of electronic communication that could be used by a Human Resources Department. Your answer must relate to a Human Resources Department. (4 KU – G)

2   Describe two benefits to the Finance Department of using a spreadsheet. Your answer must be specific to the Finance Department. (2 KU – G)

3   Explain the benefits of centralising the Administrative function in an organisation. (2 KU – C)

4   Describe two tasks undertaken by the following employees:
◆ Purchases Department Administration Assistant
◆ Human Resources Manager
◆ Wages Clerk
◆ Office Manager

Your answers must be specific to the relevant departments. (8 KU – G)

THE WORKING ENVIRONMENT: OFFICE LAYOUT

Office Layout

There are two main types of office layout that an organisation may choose to use. These are:

Cellular Office Layout

Figure 2.1 An illustration showing the layout of a cellular office

A cellular office layout can be described as an office space that has been divided up into a number of rooms of different sizes.

Each room in the office is usually only big enough for a maximum of four or five employees to work together. This means that some departments which have a lot of employees will have to use several rooms.

Within each room there will usually be a range of office equipment, such as a photocopier, a fax machine and a printer, which can be used by staff.

Although most rooms are used by departments there will be other rooms where meetings can take place or where noisy equipment is located.

An example of a room within a cellular office layout is shown on the next page.

Figure 2.2 An illustration of a room inside a cellular office

Advantages
- Rooms can be locked, meaning it is easier to maintain security.
- As there are only a few employees in each room there is less noise, so employees are not distracted.
- It is easy to hold a meeting in private as a meeting room can be used.
- Each room can be designed with the needs of each department in mind. For example, the Computing Services Department may have air conditioning installed to ensure the room does not get too hot.
- Noisy equipment such as large photocopiers can be placed in a separate room, so employees will not be distracted.

Disadvantages
- It is difficult to supervise staff as employees from the same department can be in different rooms.

- Communication can be poor or difficult because employees are in different rooms.

- If a certain department increases in size it may be impossible to move them to a bigger room or give them a second room. This means their current room will become very crowded.

- Employees, such as a reprographics assistant, can feel isolated because they are the only person in a room.

- Equipment costs can be high because each department needs its own photocopier, scanner and fax.

Open Plan Office Layout

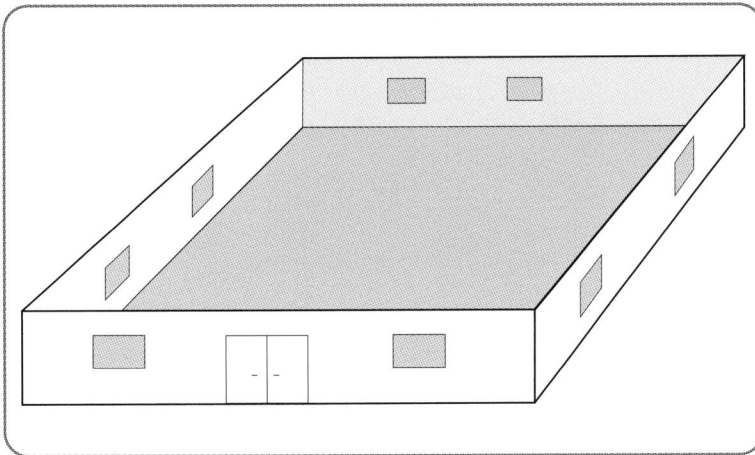

Figure 2.3 An illustration showing the layout of an open plan office

An open plan office layout can be described as one large office space where there are no rooms. Instead, moveable dividers, office furniture or plants are used to separate different departmental areas. Such offices are seen by many as being modern or flexible.

As open plan offices have no fixed walls, it is very easy to change the way the office area is designed. The open plan layout also makes it easier for staff to move about, meaning there is usually a central location where printers, scanners and faxes are located.

With there being no rooms in an open plan office, it can be difficult to hold private meetings or locate noisy equipment.

An example of an open plan office layout is shown above.

Figure 2.4 An illustration showing the layout inside an open plan office

Advantages

◆ The office space can be easily changed or altered if one department gets bigger or another gets smaller. This means better use can be made of the space available.

◆ Communication is really easy across the whole office, so meetings can be arranged quickly.

◆ Equipment such as faxes, photocopiers and scanners can be easily shared by several departments.

◆ It is easy to supervise staff as everyone is in one big office.

◆ With everybody working together and communication being better the office tends to have a friendlier atmosphere.

Disadvantages

◆ As everybody is working in the same area, it can get rather noisy, which makes it difficult for employees to concentrate.

◆ It is difficult to have a meeting in private because there may not be any rooms available.

◆ Noisy equipment can distract employees.

◆ Visitors or staff can move about the office without restriction. This means they may come across something that is confidential and which they are not meant to see.

◆ The lighting, heating and ventilation will be the same throughout the office. This may not suit certain departments or employees.

Which Office Layout Should an Organisation Use?

Choosing which office layout is the best is a difficult decision as both office designs have advantages and disadvantages. This is why in most offices there tends to be a mixture of open plan and cellular in order that the best of both worlds can be obtained.

For example, most offices will have some rooms where meetings can be held in private and where noisy equipment can be stored so it does not distract employees. A room with a locked door may also be used to store confidential information so that only those with authorisation can access it. All managers may also expect a room because they are in a senior position and often have to hold meetings or interview new members of staff.

However, in the general office space an open plan design may be used with dividers so that departmental areas can be increased or decreased in size as and when required. Making such good use of space will make it much easier to employ new staff without having to move to bigger premises. An open plan area will also make it easier for managers to supervise staff and should make it simpler for employees to communicate with each other. With equipment, such as printers, faxes and scanners being shared between areas the costs of the organisation will be lower.

Office Ergonomics (Designing an Office Where Employees Want to Work)

Most people spend a lot of their time at work sitting in an office. This is why in recent times employers have spent a considerable amount of time thinking about how to make their office space more appealing for employees. For example, employers have improved their office ergonomics by:

◆ Adding colour and pictures to the walls to make the office feel more homely and friendly.

◆ Providing good heating and air conditioning so that the office does not become too cold or hot.

◆ Using good lighting and having plenty of windows so that the office has a fresh warm feel to it.

◆ Using soundproof screens so that employees can concentrate on their work without noisy equipment distracting them.

◆ Purchasing good quality office furniture and equipment such as adjustable chairs, footrests, wrist-rests, big desks and filing cabinets which make it easier for employees to do their job.

Improving an office's ergonomics is clearly going to cost quite a lot of money. However, it has been found that improving the ergonomics of an office:

◆ Improves employees' levels of motivation and morale which should mean they produce more and better work.

◆ Makes it a safer place to work which reduces accidents and injuries.

◆ Makes it a healthier place to work which reduces staff sickness and absenteeism.

◆ Creates a positive environment which reduces stress levels and unauthorised staff absenteeism ('skiving').

Office Equipment

With the ergonomics of an office being so important it is vital that an organisation purchases good-quality office furniture which is suitable for the employees who will use it. Factors that should be taken into account when purchasing office furniture include:

Desks

Desks should have a solid and large work surface with enough space for the employee to undertake their work. There should also be room on the desk for 'in' and 'out' trays and a telephone. There should be enough space under the desk for a pedestal unit (a half-sized filing cabinet) with drawers or shelving space so that work which is not being done at present can be stored. Ideally, the desk should be easy to move so that the office space can be adjusted when necessary. It should also be a neutral colour so that it matches other furniture and maintains the ergonomics of the office.

Workstations

These are large desks that are normally set up in an L-shape. On one part of the desk a computer will be located and on the other the employee will be able to undertake their paperwork. The desk will have to be big and strong enough to hold a computer screen and keyboard. There must also be enough room for 'in' and 'out' trays and a telephone. As a computer will be on part of the desk there should be cable channels (holes) at the back of the desk so that computer wires do not become a trip hazard and the workstation looks tidy. A pedestal unit should also fit under the desk for storing filings that are currently not in use. Ideally the desk should be easy to move and adjustable so that it does not always have to be in an L-shape.

Storage Units

As most storage units are made of metal and can be locked, they are fairly secure and provide some protection in the event of a fire or a flood.

In order to keep the office neat and tidy, organisations usually purchase a variety of different-sized storage units for different purposes. Large storage units such as a bookcase can be used for storing manuals, reports and reference books. Storage cabinets on the other hand can be used for storing box files or lever arch files, whereas vertical or lateral filing cabinets are used for storing customer and employee files.

There are also a variety of smaller storage units which can be used for different purposes. For example, a multi-drawer cabinet can be used for storing paper, forms, plastic wallets and such like. A mobile pedestal unit, on the other hand, has bigger drawers and is usually placed under a desk or workstation and is used to store a stapler, a punch and files that are currently not in use.

An organisation may also purchase a card index box for storing the business cards of suppliers or customers. It may also purchase a portable metal box file for storing files which an employee removes from the office for a period of time.

Chairs

Any chair that is part of a workstation is covered under the Health and Safety (Display Screen Equipment) Regulations (1992). Under the regulations, any chair that is part of a workstation must be fully adjustable. This means that the back of the chair and the height of the chair should be adjustable to suit the needs of any employee who uses it. The chair should be on castors so that it can move and the seat should have a swivel action so the user does not have to twist and turn in the seat. The chair should be cushioned for comfort and have a stable base so that it does not tip over when in use or if somebody leans back in it.

Designing an Office Area

Although deciding to have either an open plan or a cellular office layout is important, it is also vital that consideration is given to how each area in the office should be set up.

Administrative Area

In this area you would expect to find a number of workstations where employees involved in administrative duties such as typing letters or updating databases undertake their work. The office equipment you would expect to find on the workstation would be a computer, telephone and 'in' and 'out' trays. Underneath the workstation there should be a small pedestal unit for storing files currently not in use, a stapler, paper clips, elastic bands and such like. There should also be a number of storage units, especially large ones for storing customer and employee files. The Administrative area will probably be fairly open plan so that the

Administration supervisor can keep an eye on what her team are doing. In order to improve the ergonomics of the area the walls should be pleasantly coloured, the area should be well ventilated and have good lighting.

Manager's Office

The manager's office is likely to contain a workstation with a computer, telephone and 'in' and 'out' trays. Under the workstation there should be room for a pedestal unit where papers, files and general office equipment such as a stapler or a punch can be stored. There should also be some kind of large storage unit where the manager can store files or manuals. The manager's office is likely to be in a separate room so that he can have private meetings or so he can interview people. Obviously, if he is going to do this he must make sure that he keeps his workstation free of clutter and mess. To keep things tidy and to prevent a trip hazard, all wires and cables should be bound together and the workstation should be located close to power sockets so wires do not have to lie across the floor.

An example of an ergonomically designed manager's office is shown below.

Figure 2.5 An illustration showing the layout inside a manager's office

Meeting Room or Area

A meeting room is likely to be in a separate room or be shut off from other areas using soundproof screens. In the room you would expect to find a number of desks and chairs in a circular shape so that employees can sit facing each other when having their meeting. As the room may also be used for presentations the desks and chairs should be able to be moved. The seats used should be comfortable, the walls should be painted, pictures may be attached to the walls, plants may be placed in the room and their may be tea and coffee facilities. By creating such comfortable surroundings the meeting will be conducted in a friendlier environment. Presentation ICT facilities such as a projector, laptop and screen may also be available in the room for anybody who is making a presentation.

The Modern Office and Changing Working Practices

Designing a modern office is not easy as so many different factors need to be taken into account. One of the most important in recent years has been the changing way in which people work and are employed. For example, traditionally all workers used to come into the office between 9a.m. and 5p.m. However, recently some employees and employers have requested more flexibility in working practices. This has meant that some employees have asked if they can work from home and only come into work occasionally, whereas others have asked if they can start later in the morning but finish later in the evening. Many employers have been happy to agree to this as it allows them to provide a better service to their customers.

Flexible Working Practices

Flexible working practices refer to the changing way in which people work and are employed. Flexible working practices can affect two main types of employee. The first is those workers where the employer has agreed to let the employee work away from the office. These employees are called homeworkers or teleworkers. The second is those workers who continue to work from an office.

Many pupils are unaware that flexible working practices refer to homeworking, teleworking, job share, flexitime and shift work.

Homeworking and Teleworking

Homeworking is when, for part or most of the week, an employee works from home instead of coming into the office. As you would expect, homeworking is only suitable for jobs in which the employee can carry out their job without the need to meet customers or have regular meetings with other employees. For example, journalists, designers and computer consultants can work the majority of the week from home. However, even senior managers can take advantage of homeworking

HOW TO PASS STANDARD GRADE ADMINISTRATION

as long as on a particular day they do not need to go into the office to carry out their duties.

As with homeworking, teleworking involves employees working from home. The difference between the two, however, is that unlike homeworking, a teleworker will have a direct ICT link to the office. This means that work can be sent between the employee and the office via email, fax or the telephone.

Homeworking and teleworking are often confused with each other. Although they are similar, there are key differences. Make sure you know them.

Advantages of Homeworking and Teleworking
- As some employees are working from home an employer can rent smaller premises which will save them considerable amounts of money.
- Employees avoid getting stuck in traffic when coming to work. This means less time will be lost and more work will be done which is good for the employer.
- Working from home can be less stressful and may lead to employees being more motivated. If employees are motivated, more work will be done which is good for the employer.
- Employees with disabilities may find it easier to work from home as getting to work may be difficult and time consuming.
- Employees can arrange their job around their personal circumstances. If working from home it will be easier to drop off and pick up children from school.

Specific Advantages of Teleworking
- It is easier to contact an employee if there is an ICT link to the office.
- Work can be sent to and from the employee via the ICT link.

Disadvantages of Homeworking and Teleworking
- It will be difficult for an employer to supervise staff who work from home.
- It will be difficult for an employer to run their business effectively at times. For example, calling an emergency team meeting in order to deal with an important issue will be difficult if people are working from home.
- Employees who work from home can become easily distracted and fail to complete the work they were meant to.
- The employee will miss out on the social contact of being part of an office. This may affect teamwork and cooperation within the business.

Specific Disadvantages of Teleworking
- If the ICT link between the employee and the office fails then it will be difficult for the employee to carry out their work. The employee may also fail to receive important messages about meetings.

◆ If the employee encounters ICT difficulties at home it may take longer for the problem to be sorted as they do not have a technician on site to help them.

Making Homeworking and Teleworking Work

For homeworking and teleworking to operate effectively a number of different measures need to be in place at the employee's home and at the office.

At the Employee's Home (Specific to Teleworking)

Having an ICT link to the office is clearly very important as it is the main way in which employee and employer will communicate with each other.

The simplest way to create a link is using a telephone, be that a land line or a mobile. This link can be improved if an answering machine or voicemail message facility is added to the phone, as then messages can be left even when the employer or employee are not available. However, in some instances the situation is so important that the employee must be contacted immediately. If that is the case then a pager could be used which the employee carries with them at all times and beeps if their employer wants to contact them.

Although the telephone is a good way of speaking to another person directly, sometimes the employer or the employee needs to send a written message or a particular document for the other to read. In that case a fax machine would be beneficial as the document could be sent through the fax and a direct copy would be received at the other end. Alternatively, if the employee had a personal computer (PC) or laptop at home and email access then as long as the document is in a digital format it could be emailed. The email facility could also be used for communicating messages about upcoming staff meetings or social events.

As well as offering email facilities, a laptop or PC could be connected remotely to the employer's server via a broadband connection so that the employee can access all the files that are saved on the organisation's network. Furthermore, if the PC or laptop had video conferencing software loaded and appropriate hardware (webcam, microphone) then the employee and employer would be able to have a face-to-face meeting without being in the same place.

At the Office

Although many employees may work from home, there will still be occasions when it is necessary for them to come into work, especially if they are a homeworker. This may be because they have to meet a customer or because they have a team meeting or because they have to use ICT facilities that are only available in the office.

When the employee comes into the office they will need somewhere to work. However, as such employees will not be coming in regularly, an employer will not make a desk available for all homeworkers. Instead, they will provide a small number of areas within the office where homeworkers can carry out their tasks. These include:

Hot Desk

A hot desk is a fully equipped work station (e.g. networked computer, telephone and such like) which can be booked by a homeworker in advance for use during part of the day. When the employee is finished using the hot desk, or when their booked period ends they should pack away their work so that the desk is available for the next employee who has booked it to use. An example of a hot desk is shown below.

Figure 2.6 An illustration of a Hot Desk

Hot Room

A hot room is a meeting room that a homeworker or teleworker can book in advance so that they can arrange to meet a customer at the office. The room will be private and will contain chairs, a table and tea and coffee facilities. As before, once the homeworker or teleworker has used the room they should ensure it is tidied for the next person to use.

Carrel

A carrel is a private booth that is screened on each side so that the homeworker has some privacy and can get on with their work. As with a hot desk, a carrel can be booked in advance and contains all the equipment the employee may need e.g. a desk, networked computer, telephone. An example of a carrel is shown on the next page.

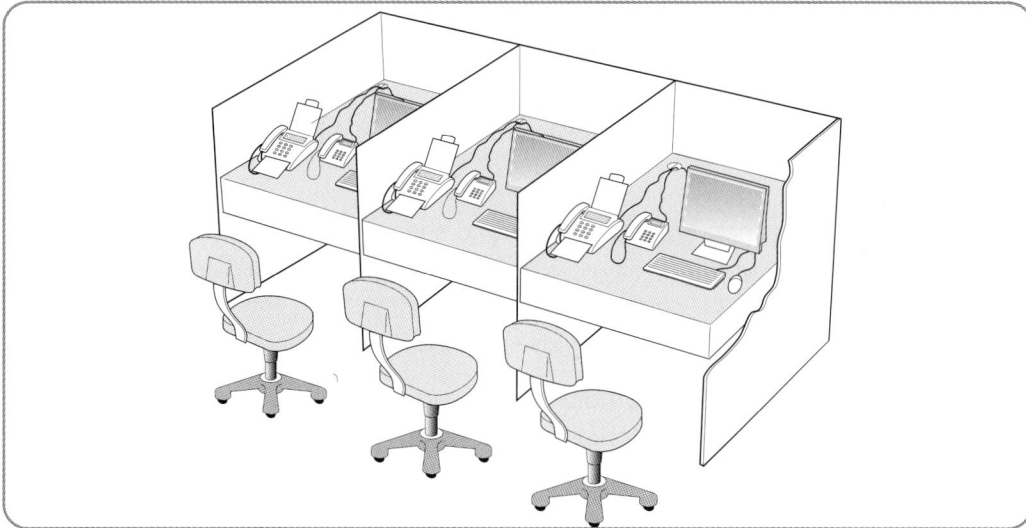

Figure 2.7 An illustration of a Carrel

Touchdown Area

A touchdown area is used by homeworkers who only need to come into the office for a very short period of time to send an email or a fax. Unlike a hot desk, a touchdown area can not be booked in advance which means a homeworker who comes into the office may have to wait before they can get onto a computer. In some organisations the touchdown area is set up like an internet café with computers and fax machines located on high tables. Stools are provided for employees to sit on whilst they work. An example of a touchdown area is shown below.

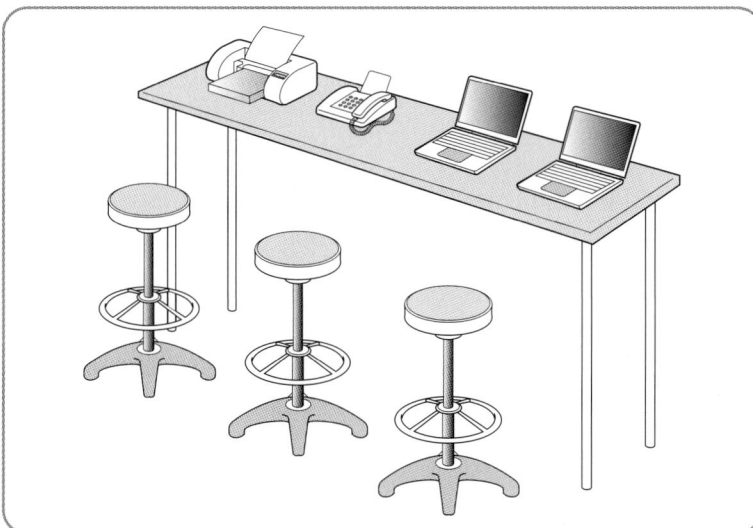

Figure 2.8 An illustration of a Touchdown Area

Employees Who Continue to Work from the Office

Although employees who work from home have been able to benefit from flexible working practices, so have employees who continue to come into the office. This has been achieved in three main ways.

Job Sharing

Job sharing involves two workers agreeing to share a full-time job. For example, one employee may work mornings, whereas the other works in the afternoon. Job share usually occurs because the employee currently doing the job no longer wishes to do it full-time and asks their employer if they can job share.

The job share is usually only authorised if someone can be found to do the hours that the current employee no longer wishes to do. If somebody is found then the employees agree what tasks and hours each will work and are paid accordingly. It is also the case that if one employee is off ill the other may be able to cover their duties until they return.

Employers are increasingly agreeing to job share because they do not want to lose good employees who would otherwise have left unless their hours were cut e.g. employees who have young children.

Flexitime

With flexitime workers are given some control over when they start and finish work. For example, an employee may decide to start work at 10a.m. and finish at 6p.m. instead of working the normal 9a.m. to 5p.m. However, although employees are given some flexibility over their start and finish times they must all be at work during certain core times during the day e.g. 11a.m. to 1p.m. These core times usually correspond to when the business is busy.

Flexitime is obviously very useful to those workers who have family commitments such as dropping off children at school as they can do that and still be on time for work. The system also allows an employee to build up extra time during the week by working longer hours so that on a Friday afternoon they can take a half day (called taking time off in lieu).

The hours that employees work and the times they start and finish are usually recorded by placing 'clocking in' and 'clocking out' cards into electronic recording equipment.

Many employers have introduced flexitime as giving employees more flexibility over when they work tends to make them happier and keener to work. Unauthorised absences also fall as employees will be far less likely to take a day off because they have an appointment at the doctors or because a gas or electric engineer is due to arrive.

Shift Work

Shift work is used by organisations that are open 24 hours a day e.g. a telephone call centre, a supermarket or a car manufacturer. As no employee is able to work for 24 hours continuously without a break the day is split up into three 8-hour shifts. Employees are then given a particular shift which they work for a certain period of time, say a week to a month, before they are moved onto a different shift.

As working the night shift is often unpopular with employees, an employer will pay workers extra for doing that shift.

Shift work does provide some flexibility to employees as a worker can request that they are always on a particular shift. For example, a father may request a night shift so that he can look after his children while his wife is at work during the day. It may also be possible for workers to swap shifts as long as they have had the swap agreed by their employer.

Shift work has been introduced by many employers as it allows them to produce products 24 hours a day which means the business is making money all the time. Having the business open 24 hours a day also allows the organisation to provide a better service to their customers as people can purchase or contact the business whenever they want.

Questions

1 Suggest two problems which may be associated with working in an open plan office. (2 KU – C)

2 Justify the use of two types of ICT equipment used by teleworkers. A different justification must be given for each item of equipment. (2 KU – C)

3 Justify the use of hot rooms and carrels in modern offices. (4 KU – C)

4 Describe three actions which could be taken by Highlife Ltd to solve each of the problems below. Each action must be different.

♦ A number of experienced staff have left because their full-time jobs do not give them enough time with their newly born babies.

♦ A number of employees who work from home have complained that there are no facilities available to them when they come into the office.

♦ A homeworker recently missed an important meeting at the office as he was not aware of it. (3 PS – G)

THE WORKING ENVIRONMENT: SAFE WORKING PRACTICES

Health and Safety

Although taking Health and Safety seriously may not be cool, it is one of the most important issues that an organisation needs to address.

Accidents can happen anywhere in an office. This is why it is vital that regular health and safety checks are undertaken in order to identify potential hazards in the office. Potential hazards are anything in an office environment, for example equipment or the way people work, that may cause an accident to occur in the future. If such potential hazards can be identified then time can be spent rectifying the problem before it causes an accident and someone gets injured.

Below is an example of an office environment where health and safety is not being taken seriously. It is only a matter of time before someone gets seriously injured.

Figure 2.9 An illustration of a dangerous office

What Potential Hazards do Employees Encounter in an Office?

Identifying potential hazards can be difficult as sometimes something does not seem to be a problem until an accident actually happens. This is why it is important to have an understanding of what types of accidents can occur when undertaking a health and safety check of an office.

However, equally important is to make any potential hazards that are found safe before they cause any danger.

Hints and Tips

When providing a solution to a problem it is not enough to just say 'do not do that'. You must provide an actual solution to the problem. See below for some examples.

Example

Examples of potential hazards and how they may be solved include:

Potential Hazard 1: Wires from computers or other equipment lying across the floor which employees could trip over.

Solution 1: The computers or equipment could be moved closer to power sockets so that wires do not have to trail across the floor. If this is not possible, all the wires should be placed in a cable tidy which is then highlighted with hazard tape so that it can be easily seen.

Potential Hazard 2: Locking or blocking a fire door exit, meaning people cannot escape during a fire.

Solution 2: Make sure a sign is placed on the fire door stating that the door must never be locked and the area must always be kept free and clear. All employees should also be made aware of this.

Potential Hazard 3: A fire door being left open or ajar. This would allow a fire to spread throughout a building.

Solution 3: Place a sign on the door instructing all employees to keep the fire door shut at all times. All employees should also be made aware of this.

Potential Hazard 4: Employees without qualifications trying to repair equipment which may give them an electric shock or injure them.

Example continued ➤

Example *continued*

Solution 4: If electrical equipment breaks down the item should be turned off and a notice attached to it saying it is currently out of use. A qualified engineer should then be phoned in order that the piece of equipment can be repaired.

Potential Hazard 5: Employees receiving an electric shock when opening electrical equipment, such as a printer to replace an ink cartridge, remove a paper jam or to insert new paper.

Solution 5: Advise employees to always switch equipment off at the socket before opening it.

Potential Hazard 6: Split water being left in a walkway which may cause an employee to slip and fall.

Solution 6: A wet floor sign should be placed over the spillage until it is mopped up and dried.

Potential Hazard 7: A badly set up workstation causing an employee to suffer from back pain or repetitive strain injury (RSI).

Solution 7: Make sure chairs are fully adjustable and that appropriate footrests and wrist-rests are given to employees who use computer equipment.

Potential Hazard 8: Poor lighting or flickering lights causing employees to suffer from eye strain and headaches.

Solution 8: Ensure all light bulbs are replaced when they stop working or provide employees with desk lights.

Potential Hazard 9: Glare from the Sun causing computer operators to suffer from eye strain and headaches.

Solution 9: Fit all computer screens with glare guards or have blinds on every window so that the glare from the Sun can be shut out.

Potential Hazard 10: The heat or noise in a room causing employees to suffer from headaches and tiredness.

Solution 10: Make sure the room has a ventilation system that can be adjusted to ensure a constant temperature. Put noisy equipment in a separate room from employees.

Potential Hazard 11: Only filling the top drawer of a filing cabinet will make it unstable and likely to tip over and fall on an employee.

Example *continued* ➤

Example *continued*

Solution 11: Advise employees to fill filing cabinets from the bottom up.

Potential Hazard 12: Flammable items such as paper being stored close to open gas heaters.

Solution 12: Make sure flammable items are not placed close to open flames. Replace open flame heaters with radiators. Make sure the office has enough fire extinguishers.

Potential Hazard 13: Boxes or deliveries being left in the middle of walkways which people may fall over or knock into.

Solution 13: All boxes or deliveries should be placed in a designated storage area until someone is ready to unpack the contents.

Potential Hazard 14: Employees trying to carry equipment or files which are too heavy or big meaning they are likely to fall or trip.

Solution 14: Provide employees with guidance or training on what they are allowed to carry without help.

Potential Hazard 15: Electrical equipment being stored close to liquid or liquid being left on top of electrical equipment. If spilt, the liquid may cause the electrical equipment to short circuit.

Solution 15: Move electrical equipment away from where liquids are stored or kept. Advise employees to never place liquids on top of electrical equipment.

What Potential Hazards and Health Problems do Employees Encounter when using Computer Equipment?

In most modern offices, a significant number of employees will spend a considerable amount of their day working on a computer. This, however, can cause a number of health problems for such employees.

As you would expect, staring at a screen all day tires your eyes out and as a result may cause eyestrain and associated headaches. These problems are made even worse if the screen the operator is using is not working properly or if the conditions under which the employee works are not good. For example, if the screen flickers or has a poor resolution the operator will find it difficult to see what is on the screen causing health problems for the employee. Similarly, if the Sun is able to glare against the operator's screen or the lighting in the room is poor or the room is just too hot, health problems will also occur.

It is very important that appropriate action is taken to prevent health problems related to using display screen equipment. First, the operator should be given appropriate health and safety training on how to use the equipment and advised that regular breaks should be taken. For example, employees should be shown how to adjust their computer screen so that the display is clear and in focus. Measures should also be in place to provide operators with regular eye tests. Rooms in which computer operators work should be properly ventilated, lit and have blinds at every window in order to prevent the glare from the Sun.

Members of staff who regularly use computers may also suffer from Repetitive Strain Injury, or RSI, as the constant tapping on a keyboard eventually tires out your finger and wrist joints. Computer operators can also suffer from back aches and other associated pains caused by typing on a keyboard all day while sitting in a more or less fixed position.

To overcome these strain injury problems it is important to give staff advice and training on how to set up and adjust their chair. Of course the chair that an employee is given should be fully adjustable and provide sufficient support for the operator's back and upper legs. Wrist-rests and footrests should also be provided so that areas that come under strain are supported appropriately.

It is also important that the employee sets out their workstation appropriately so that they can work comfortably. For example, an employee should consider where and at what height their keyboard, mouse, screen and printer will be located on their desk. Equally important, the operator must also think about how they will position themselves. For example, their eye level should be at the same height as the computer screen. The employee should sit facing onto their computer screen with their upper and lower arms at approximately right angles when typing.

Although setting up a workstation correctly and making sure an operator is positioned correctly can reduce RSIs and other pains it will not eliminate them completely. This is why it is important that employees should take regular breaks where they can move about and ease any strains that may be developing.

Working with computers can also be extremely stressful. Learning to use new technology or software can be difficult and frustrating, whereas old computer equipment that continually breaks down or software that crashes can be very annoying to an employee. To the same degree, many keyboard operators have very repetitive jobs which can become boring, while others have very demanding jobs where the workload is extremely heavy.

To prevent such problems it is absolutely vital that employees are always given training in how to use new technology and software. Old technology and software that is unreliable should be repaired or replaced with equipment that works. If possible, employees should be given varied tasks and supervisors should make sure that an employee's workload is not too great.

What Safety Procedure Should Employees Follow?

Although regular health and safety checks may be undertaken by an organisation there will still be times when an employee identifies a potential hazard in their day-to-day work. For example, some water may be spilt in the middle of a walkway or a computer screen may begin to smoke.

The one thing that an employee should not do is ignore the problem. Potential hazards do not go away and in fact have a nasty habit of causing serious accidents. Equally important, the employee should not attempt to sort the problem out, especially if it is a fault with electrical or mechanical equipment.

Instead, all an employee should do is try to make the area as safe as possible without putting themselves in danger. For example, this would mean turning electrical equipment off at the socket and then putting a sign on the machine that notes it has developed a fault and should not be used. If there is anybody else in the room, then the employee should tell them as well. If, however, some water had been split in a walkway, then the employee should ask someone to stand by the slip hazard until they are able to place a hazard sign beside it or until a janitor has been called to clear it up.

The absolute key in any situation is to make the situation as safe as possible as quickly as possible without putting yourself in danger. Once that has been done, a hazard/fault report form should be completed which should then be passed to either your line manager or your health and safety officer. They will then contact the relevant repair person e.g. janitor, maintenance engineer in order to have the fault sorted out.

Safety Procedure

1   Do not ignore the problem.
2   Make the area as safe as possible without putting yourself in danger.
3   Complete a Hazard Report Form (see below) immediately and pass to your line manager.
4   Line manager will contact appropriate individual in order that the problem can be resolved.

41

HAZARD/FAULT REPORT FORM	
Location	Finance Department
Describe the Hazard/Fault	The fire door was blocked by a number of empty cardboard boxes.
Action taken if any	Boxes removed and placed down by the recycling bins.
Reported by	Kenny Leese
Date	10/6/08
Pass the completed form to your immediate supervisor.	

Emergency Safety Procedures

Although an organisation may undertake regular health and safety checks and staff report potential hazards as and when they identify them, there is still no getting away from the fact that accidents will happen in the workplace. Worse still, in some circumstances the accident will be serious. In order to deal with such circumstances, organisations have in place emergency safety procedures which go beyond the basic safety procedure described in the section above. Two such situations would be if an employee got injured at work and if there was a fire in the workplace.

Injured Person

As employees sometimes get injured at work many organisations train staff in basic first aid and have a designated employee who has been on an approved Health and Safety Executive first aid course.

In the event of an accident, a trained first aider should be called and if the accident is serious the emergency services as well. While waiting for the first aider to arrive, it is important that the injured person be told that help is on its way and that whoever is with them tries to keep the injured person calm by talking to them. Under no circumstances should an employee without first aid training attempt to help the injured person as they are likely to do more harm than good. The employee who finds the injured person should only leave the scene once a trained first aider arrives.

Shortly after an accident, and while everything is still fresh in the mind of the employee who found the injured person, an Accident Report Form should be completed. The core details from the Accident Report Form should then be entered into the Accident Book which records all accidents that have taken place in the business. It is important that both these documents are maintained accurately because if the Health and Safety Executive visit the organisation they will ask to inspect such documents.

Fire in the Building

If an employee discovers a fire the first thing they should do is warn others in the immediate area. After that the employee should then go to the nearest fire alarm point and sound the fire alarm. On hearing the fire alarm, a designated employee, sometimes called the fire officer, will phone the emergency services to request the Fire Brigade.

Attempts should only be made to contain the fire if employees in the area of the fire have been properly trained to use the fire extinguishing equipment that is available. However, under no circumstances should any employee put themselves in unnecessary danger. The first rule is always – safety first.

If the fire can not be contained the door to the room in which the fire is taking place should be closed, and if possible, the windows inside as well. This is so the fire will have difficulty spreading to other areas.

On hearing the fire alarm all employees and visitors must leave the building by the nearest fire exit. All visitors should be accompanied by an employee when leaving the building so that they do not get lost or disorientated. In some organisations, certain employees will be designated to direct others to the nearest fire exit.

Under absolutely no circumstances should anyone use a lift because if the fire burns through electrics or gets into the lift well the lift may stop working and employees will be in severe danger. It is also important that no one stops to put on coats or collect personal belongings as such delays may allow the fire to spread and prevent employees being able to leave by the fire exit.

Although a fire evacuation can be frightening it is vital that people do not run, panic or push as this may cause an accident which actually slows down the evacuation.

Once out of the building it is important that employees and visitors make their way to the fire assembly point where a roll call will be taken. The roll call will usually be taken by the head receptionist who will have brought out a list of all those who are currently in the building.

In order that staff are fully aware of an organisation's fire evacuation procedure, notices outlining the procedure are displayed throughout the building. On each notice, the nearest fire exit should be noted along with the appropriate fire assembly point for that part of the building. In addition, organisations will also run practise fire drills so that everyone knows exactly what to do in the event of a real fire.

ACCIDENT REPORT FORM	
Name of injured person	Lee Cooper
Date and time of accident	Thursday, 12 June 2008 at 1345 hours
Give a brief description of the accident	Lee tripped and fell on a trailing wire from a photocopier.
Place of accident	Reprographics Room
Details of injury	Bruised knee and strained wrist
Give details of first aid treatment given	Wrist strapped
Was the injured person taken to hospital?	No
Reported by	Ian Conn
Date	23/7/08

On completion this form should be passed to the Health and Safety Officer.

ACCIDENT BOOK					
Date	Time	Location	Name of Injured person	Witness	Details of Accident and Action Taken
18/7/08	1115 hours	HR Department	Kerry Jones	Paul Peep	Filing cabinet fell on top of her. Arm broken. Taken to hospital.
23/7/08	1345 hours	Reprographics Room	Lee Cooper	Ian Conn	Tripped over trailing wire from a photocopier. Bruised knee and strained wrist. Wrist strapped.

Effective First Aid

While on their first aid course, a first aider will be trained in the basic use of a first aid box. Within the box the following items should be found:

◆ A leaflet providing general first aid advice

◆ Disposable gloves

◆ Safety pins

◆ Bandages and unmedicated dressings of various sizes

◆ Plasters of various sizes

◆ Sterile eye pads.

It is important to note that tablets and medicines should not be kept in a first aid box. Such items should only ever be administered by a trained medical practitioner.

Health and Safety Legislation

Health and Safety in the workplace has become an increasingly important issue since the 1960s. To ensure that Health and Safety is taken seriously and to make sure all organisations follow certain standards a number of laws have been passed which cover certain key areas.

Health and Safety at Work Act (HASAWA) (1974)

This Act is the key piece of legislation covering health and safety in the workplace. Interestingly, it places responsibility for health and safety in the hands of both employer and employee. This is important as it makes the point that health and safety is a shared responsibility.

Under the Act, employers are responsible for maintaining safe working conditions and safe working methods. This involves, making sure that:

◆ Entrances and exits to the workplace are safe

◆ Equipment is safe and properly maintained

◆ Regular health and safety checks are undertaken to ensure a safe working environment

◆ Protective clothing is provided where necessary

◆ Dangerous substances are properly stored and used according to instructions

◆ Employees are given adequate health and safety training so that they can carry out their duties safely

◆ The organisation has a health and safety policy that all employees are made aware of

Employees are responsible for, making sure that:

- They carry out their duties in a safe manner and without putting other employees in danger
- They follow the health and safety procedures of the organisation
- They use any health and safety equipment or protective clothing as they have been trained to do so
- They work with the employer to ensure good health and safety in the workplace.

Hints and Tips

Make sure you know what employers and employees responsibilities are with regard to maintaining a healthy and safe working environment. It is a common exam question that is often answered poorly.

Health and Safety (First Aid) Regulations (1981)

These regulations cover first aid arrangements in an organisation and in particular making sure that should a first aid situation arise, it is dealt with effectively.

The regulations state that an employer must appoint someone to be in charge of first aid arrangements within an organisation. The person appointed will also be responsible for making sure the first aid box is suitably maintained and stocked with the equipment needed.

The organisation must also make sure that a designated first aider is appointed who will attend to any injured person should an incident occur. The designated first aider can also be the person who has been appointed to be in charge of an organisation's first aid arrangements.

Should an accident occur, the regulations state that a permanent record should be kept of the incident. For example, the details of the incident should be recorded on an accident report form and in the accident book

To ensure that an incident is dealt with quickly, all employees should be made aware of first aid arrangements such as where first aid boxes are kept and who the designated first aider is.

Health and Safety (Display Screen Equipment) Regulations (1992)

These regulations were introduced in response to the increasing number of employees who use display screen equipment as part of their day-to-day job.

Under the regulations, employers are responsible for making sure that workstations are assessed in terms of their health and safety. This would involve regular checks of equipment, furniture and the general working environment to make sure they at least meet minimum requirements. Employers should also provide their employees with training on how adjustments can be made to their workstation areas and display screens in order that health and safety problems can be avoided.

The regulations also state that employees who use display screen equipment throughout the day must be given sufficient rest breaks or a variety of tasks to do. Such employees are also entitled to regular eye tests which the employer must pay for. If it is discovered that an employee who regularly uses display screen equipment needs spectacles then the employer will be responsible for paying for the glasses.

Reporting of Injuries, Diseases and Dangerous Occurrences Regulations (RIDDOR) (1995)

These regulations deal with incidents that occur at a workplace and in particular how such incidents should be recorded and who should be notified of any such events.

If an accident occurs that causes death or major injury then the relevant enforcing authority must be contacted immediately and an accident report form should be completed and forwarded to them within 10 days.

If the injury is not major but prevents an employee working for more than 3 days an accident report form should be forwarded to the relevant enforcing authority within 10 days.

In the event of a doctor informing an employer that one of their employees is suffering from a reportable work-related disease, the employer must forward a disease report form to the relevant enforcing authority within 10 days.

Even if an employee is uninjured, dangerous occurrences should be reported to the relevant enforcing authority immediately and an accident report form should be completed and forwarded within 10 days.

All accident report forms should be kept by an organisation for a minimum of 3 years after the date of the incident. On each form, the date, time and place of the incident should be detailed along with how and why the incident occurred, and who was involved.

Questions

1   Suggest an appropriate solution to each of the following problems. Each solution must be different.

   ◆ When a small fire occurred recently, staff discovered that the fire exit was locked.

   ◆ A member of staff received an electric shock from a photocopier when trying to remove a paper jam.

   ◆ A member of staff was injured after tripping over a trailing wire from a telephone.

   ◆ A computer was destroyed after a glass of water was spilt over it. (4 PS – G)

2   Suggest three actions that could be taken to ensure employees who work regularly with computer equipment avoid health problems. (3 PS – G)

3   An Administration Assistant has just noticed some smoke coming from a photocopier. Suggest and justify appropriate safety procedures that should be followed. (4 PS – C)

4   Employees have a responsibility to ensure that the workplace is a healthy and safe environment. Explain how an employee could achieve this. (3 KU – C)

5   Explain two responsibilities that employers have to ensure that the working environment their employees work in is safe. (2 KU – C)

THE WORKING ENVIRONMENT: RECEPTION SERVICES

A Receptionist

Feet on the desk, cigarette in mouth and with an attitude like an angry hippopotamus is exactly what you do not want in a receptionist. As the first person a visitor will meet when entering an organisation it is absolutely vital that a receptionist gives a positive impression. This is why it is essential that a receptionist has certain characteristics and qualities.

Qualities and Characteristics of a Good Receptionist

Being polite and friendly to visitors is only one part of being an effective receptionist. In fact, to be really good at the job, a receptionist should have a clear voice so that they can be easily understood when speaking to visitors. Having the ability to remain calm and patient is also important. For example, when dealing with a difficult visitor, a receptionist would only make the situation worse if they lost their temper. More often than not, remaining calm will help to cool the situation down.

Looking well presented is also important, as being the first person that a visitor sees it is vital that a positive impression of the organisation is given. This also means that the receptionist should keep their work area tidy at all times so that the organisation looks organised and professional. Important documents that are used frequently, such as a Visitors' Book and a Staff Signing In/Out Book, should be kept close at hand so that the receptionist can deal with such situations quickly and effectively.

A receptionist must also be able to deal with basic queries and have a good knowledge of who works in the business and in which department they work. This is important, as visitors quickly get a bad impression of a business if the receptionist is unable to answer any questions or is unable to contact who they want to speak to. To avoid such problems it is important that a receptionist has a list of basic information that is frequently requested close at hand. For example, a list of all employees' names, their departmental location and telephone extensions would be beneficial. An organisation chart on the wall would also be useful as it would allow the receptionist to refer to it when answering a visitor's query. Similarly, having a range of organisational leaflets, a catalogue of products and price lists would also be useful when dealing with basic visitor queries.

The Duties of a Receptionist

As the public face of an organisation, a receptionist is responsible for welcoming visitors to the organisation and putting them at ease. As part of that process, the receptionist will take the visitor's name and advise the relevant employee that their appointment has arrived.

Before the visitor enters the main part of the building, the receptionist will enter their details in the Visitors' Book and provide them with a visitors' pass. After that they will direct the visitor to the waiting area or take them to the office of the person they are here to see.

As well as dealing with visitors, a receptionist will be involved in answering phone calls. If it is a large organisation the receptionist may operate a switchboard which will allow them to transfer calls to employees. If there is no transfer system in place the receptionist will take messages and pass them on to the relevant employee.

In order to maintain a positive image, a receptionist will also be responsible for making sure that the reception area and waiting area are kept tidy and well presented. This means picking up any litter that may have been dropped on the floor; tidying away any coffee cups and magazines left scattered about the waiting area as well as watering plants.

From time to time, the receptionist will be responsible for signing for parcels or recorded mail which is delivered to the office. In any free time that the receptionist has left they may type up letters or undertake other minor administrative duties.

How are Staff and Visitors Registered at Reception?

As a receptionist is the first person a visitor or a member of staff meets when they enter the building and the last person they see when they leave the building it is important that a number of registration records are kept and maintained at reception.

Staff Signing-In Book

A Staff Signing-In Book is used by staff every day when they first enter the building. As the example below shows, the employee enters their time of arrival, their name and which department they are from.

STAFF SIGNING-IN BOOK		
Date: Wednesday 25 July 2008		**Receptionist:** John Barr
Time In	**Name**	**Department**
0830	Brian Jerr	Finance
0835	Kim Low	Human Resources

A Staff Signing-In Book is clearly important as it will provide an accurate record of which members of staff are in the building and when they arrived. This is not only important as a means of checking on an employee's time keeping, but also in the event of an emergency, such as fire, when it is essential to know who is in the building.

Staff In/Out Book

A Staff Signing-In Book is only useful in an emergency if used with a Staff In/Out Book. This is because in the event of an emergency or evacuation it is important to know who is in the building at that time. If this were not known, the fire service may enter the building and put themselves in unnecessary danger looking for people who are not there. This is why a Staff In/Out Book should be used when an employee leaves the building to go out for their lunch, or to visit a customer. As the example below shows, the member of staff records in the Staff In/Out Book the time they leave and the time they return.

STAFF IN/OUT BOOK				
Date: Wednesday 25 July 2008			**Receptionist:** John Barr	
Time Out	**Name**	**Department**	**Gone To**	**Time In**
1015	Jill Potts	Sales & Marketing	Jarvie Ltd	1245
1205	John Jones	Admin	Lunch	1300

Appointments' Book

An Appointments' Book is used by the receptionist to keep a record of all the appointments that have been made for a particular day. It is essential that if a manager makes an appointment with someone that they record the details in the book or tell the receptionist to do so. If not, the receptionist will be caught off guard when an appointment arrives and will have to check with the manager that the appointment exists. Worse still though, is when two appointments are booked at the same time with the same manager. This can happen if someone forgets to record an appointment and then someone else makes an appointment at the same time thinking it is free. A manager should also advise a receptionist if there are any times when appointments should not be made so the receptionist does not pencil in any appointments for those times.

The details that are recorded in an Appointments' Book are the time of the appointment, the name of the person who called, the name of the organisation they are from and the name of the person they are to visit.

APPOINTMENTS' BOOK			
Date: Wednesday 25 July 2008		**Receptionist:** John Barr	
Time	**Name of Appointment**	**Name of the Organisation**	**To See**
1000	Mr L Kent	Donside Windows	Mr I Lions
1115	Miss D Gorr	FGV Recruitment	Mrs F Henderson

Electronic Diary – A Modern Appointments' Book

In many modern organisations, appointments and the arranging of meetings occur electronically. Instead of making an entry in an appointments' book, the receptionist will input the information directly into a manager's electronic diary, such as Microsoft Outlook. For such a system to work effectively all the computers in an organisation must be networked and the receptionist must have authority to access each manager's electronic diary.

Using an electronic diary over a paper-based appointments' book has many advantages. For example, it is much easier to make changes to an electronic diary should the details of an appointment or meeting change. It is also easier for a receptionist to make and arrange appointments or meetings. Instead of having to phone a manager to make sure an appointment time is suitable, the receptionist can check their electronic diary and make the appointment if the time is free. The same is also true when arranging a meeting for a number of different staff. Instead of having to phone each one individually, the receptionist can check their electronic diaries to see when everyone is free and then schedule the meeting. Better still, if the meeting occurs on a regular basis, the receptionist can set up the diary entry so that the details are automatically entered into the diary at the same time every week or month.

A receptionist can also use the electronic diary to check in appointments when they arrive. By accessing a particular manager's electronic diary, the receptionist can confirm the appointment before contacting the manager to let them know their appointment has arrived.

An electronic diary is also of great benefit to a manager as it is much easier for them to detail times when they are not available for appointments by making an appropriate entry in their electronic diary. Further still, if they make an appointment directly with a customer all they need to do is enter the details into their electronic diary. By doing this, the horrible situation of two appointments being booked for the same time is avoided. This is because an electronic diary will not allow a receptionist to book an appointment at a time that has already been taken.

An electronic diary also allows more detail to be entered when an appointment is being made. For example, details of important papers that need to be taken to a particular meeting can be listed against the entry so that the manager does not forget. Using an electronic diary also makes it easier for a manager to prepare for a meeting or an appointment by providing an electronic reminder, say 15 minutes before the meeting or the visitor is due to arrive. This gives the manager time to gather all the papers they will need before the meeting begins or appointment arrives.

Visitors' Book

A Visitors' Book is used by a receptionist to maintain a record of all people who visit the organisation. Only those people who are to go beyond the reception area will have their details recorded. Those people, such as postal workers, who are just dropping something off do not record their details in the Visitors' Book.

Maintaining an accurate Visitors' Book is important as it shows if there are any visitors in the building at a particular time of day. This is obviously important in the event of an emergency, when it is essential to know who is in the building. It is also useful at the end of the day when the building is being locked up. If a visitor has not signed out it lets the receptionist know that they are still in the building.

The details that are recorded in a Visitors' Book are the name of the visitor, the name of the organisation they are from, their car registration number, the visitor badge number they are given, the name of the person they are here to visit, and their arrival and departure times. Recording these details is useful as sometimes the visitor may need to be contacted while in the building because their car needs to be moved or because someone from their business has called.

VISITORS' BOOK						
Date: Wednesday 25 July 2008			**Receptionist:** John Barr			
Name	**Organisation**	**Car Reg**	**Badge No**	**To See**	**Arrive**	**Depart**
L Kent	Donside Windows	SY07 9TY	1	I Lions	0955	1045
Dee Gorr	FGV Recruitment	SF57 6GD	2	F Henderson	1110	1230

Dealing with Visitors

One of the main responsibilities that a receptionist will have is dealing with visitors. In general, this involves being polite and friendly so the visitor feels welcomed. More specifically though, it involves following a set procedure so that the visitor is dealt with in a professional way.

When a visitor arrives at reception it is important to ask their name, what organisation they are from, who they are here to see and whether they have an appointment or not.

Visitor with an Appointment

If the visitor has an appointment then their name and details should be checked off in the Appointments' Book. After that, the visitor should be asked to sign the Visitors' Book while the receptionist prepares a visitor's badge. With the visitor's details having now been taken the receptionist should phone the manager they are here to see to let them know that their appointment has arrived.

If the visitor has arrived early or the manager they are here to see is slightly delayed it may be necessary for the receptionist to take the visitor to the waiting area. While there the receptionist should offer the visitor a seat and ask them whether they would like a cup of tea or coffee. On the other hand, if the manager is ready to see their appointment the receptionist should either accompany the visitor to the manager's office or ask them to wait until the manager comes down to collect them.

Visitor without an Appointment

In some instances a visitor to an organisation may not have an appointment. If that is the case the receptionist should ask the visitor who they wish to see and why. The receptionist should then ask the visitor to take a seat in the waiting area while they contact the manager and ask them if they are available to see the visitor.

If the manager is available, the visitor should be asked to complete the Visitors' Book while the receptionist prepares a visitors' badge. Once this has been done, the receptionist should then accompany the visitor to the manager's office or ask them to take a seat in the waiting area until the manager comes to collect them.

If the manager is not available, the receptionist should apologise to the visitor and then ask if an appointment could be made for a later date or if someone else in the organisation could assist instead.

The Reception Area

As the reception area is often seen as the face of an organisation, a considerable amount of time and money is spent on making sure that it is designed effectively and runs smoothly. The four most important factors that should be taken into account are:

◆ The Needs of the Receptionist

◆ Creating a Positive Public Image

◆ The Needs of Visitors

◆ The Need for Good Security.

Receptionist

As the receptionist is responsible for welcoming visitors and keeping an eye on the reception area it is important that their desk is positioned close to the front entrance. Having a big reception desk close to the front entrance will also let visitors know exactly where to go when they step inside the building, especially if the receptionist acknowledges the visitor by giving them eye contact and a friendly smile.

On the receptionist's desk there should be sufficient room for a Staff Signing-In Book, a Staff In/Out Book, a Visitors' Book and an Appointments' Book. There should also be storage areas under the desk for visitors' badges and files so that the desk can be kept tidy at all times. There may also be a storage unit behind the receptionist where catalogues, price lists and other brochures are stored. It is important that every item needed by the receptionist should be close at hand so that they do not need to leave their desk unattended. There are only a few things that convey a worse image than an organisation that leaves its reception area unattended. This is why there should be a rota in place to cover any periods such as lunchtime when the receptionist is away from their desk. Whoever takes over for that short period of time should be given enough training to do the job effectively.

On the desk there should be a phone and a computer. The phone will be used to contact employees when visitors arrive and the computer may be used to carry out administrative duties or to update the Appointments' Book if it is stored on the PC.

In large organisations, where there is more than one receptionist, there may be a switchboard, through which one of the receptionists will answer calls and then forward them onto the appropriate employee. There may also be a public address system which the receptionist can use to contact employees who are in the building, but away from their desk.

Positive Public Image

It is important that a reception area is clean, well decorated and looks modern. This means that the flooring, walls and work surfaces must be kept clean and tidy at all times.

The flooring used should be durable and resistant to stains as so many people will be walking across it. The walls should be well decorated in light neutral colours with paintings attached in order to add colour. An organisation chart containing pictures of senior managers should also be displayed on the wall. Alongside the organisation chart the organisation may display certificates and awards, such as Investors in People, to let visitors know that they are a professional organisation.

Lighting in the reception area should be good and cover every corner through the use of spotlights. In order to maintain a constant temperature the area should have an adjustable heating and ventilation system. Plants may also be positioned around the reception area in order to convey a friendly and relaxed atmosphere.

The entrance to the reception area should be open and wide enough for a disabled person to enter with ease. Automatic glass doors may be used to aid access and to provide natural light into the reception area.

An example of a reception area is shown below.

Figure 2.10 An illustration of a reception area in an office

Visitors

In order that visitors do not get lost, signs are usually placed in the visitors' car park and on any pathways into the organisation which direct visitors to the reception area.

The reception area should be fairly large and have a waiting area for visitors. In the waiting area there should be comfortable chairs and a table on top of which there should be a range of reading material, such as organisational brochures and magazines. The waiting area should be well decorated in light neutral colours with paintings attached to the walls and plants located throughout in order to provide a friendly relaxed feel. Tea and coffee facilities as well as a water cooler should be provided so that a visitor can have a drink while they are waiting.

Close by there should be toilet facilities with disabled access so that a visitor can freshen up before their meeting.

An example of a visitors' area is shown below.

Figure 2.11 An illustration of a waiting area in an office

Security

The main reception area should be the only way in which a visitor can enter the organisation's building. All other access doors should either be locked or require a security swipe card in order to enter via them. In some organisations, usually those that share premises with other businesses or where the reception area is up a flight of stairs from the entrance, an entry phone system may operate. With such a system, any visitor to the organisation must press a buzzer at the front entrance which attracts the attention of the receptionist. The receptionist can then ask the visitor who they are and who they are here to see before pressing a button that unlocks the door remotely and allows the visitor access.

As so many visitors and staff pass through the reception area it is essential that all employees wear a security ID (identification) badge which is on clear display and has a picture of them on it. This is so the receptionist can quickly and easily identify a member of staff from a visitor and hence let the employee enter the main office after signing the Staff Signing-In Book. In some large organisations, a security guard may be employed to check ID badges and ensure that only those who are authorised gain access to the main office. In certain buildings, for example, the Houses of Parliament, a security guard may be employed to search the bags and briefcases of employees and visitors as they enter and leave the building.

If a security ID badge is not worn, the individual should be stopped until it can be verified that they are an employee. Under no circumstances should anyone without a security ID badge be allowed through reception and into the main office as from there it is a lot easier to gain access to private and confidential information.

The reception desk should be manned at all times so that visitors have someone to approach as soon as they enter the building and also because it acts as a visual deterrent to anyone who might want to cause trouble. When a visitor enters the building, the receptionist should acknowledge them with a smile or a hello. Although this is polite, it also lets the visitor know that their presence has been noted. After approaching the reception desk, the visitor should be asked how they can be helped. If they are here to see someone their name should be checked off against the Appointments' Book and then issued with a visitors' badge as they complete the Visitors' Book. By providing the visitor with a badge, staff inside the building will then know that the visitor has authority to be there.

After issuing the visitor with a badge, the receptionist should either accompany the visitor to the manager's office or direct the visitor to take a seat in the waiting area until a manager arrives to collect them. The visitor should never be allowed to wander around inside the building unattended.

If for some reason the desk cannot be manned at all times then all doors off the reception area should be protected by locked doors that can only be opened by swiping a security card through a reader or inputting a keypad number that is only known to staff. By doing this, visitors will be unable to just wander into the main office without appropriate authority.

It would also be prudent to install CCTV cameras in the reception area as it is impossible for a receptionist to keep an eye on everything all of the time. By using CCTV, any incident that happens in the reception area can be played back in order to ascertain exactly what happened.

Security Procedures

Although not all security problems can be anticipated, there are number that can be. In order that that they are dealt with effectively, an organisation may develop procedures which set out exactly how each situation should be dealt with. Some common incidents that may be encountered by a receptionist are noted below.

Aggressive Visitor

From time to time a visitor may become aggressive towards the receptionist of an organisation. If this occurs, it is essential that the receptionist remain composed while they try to calm the visitor down using a soft voice and non-aggressive body language. Under no circumstances should the receptionist try to restrain or grab the visitor as this may agitate them further.

If the visitor refuses to calm down, the receptionist should call for security in order that the visitor can be removed from the premises safely. Should the visitor be from another organisation, they should be informed of his behaviour so that they can reprimand their employee on his return.

In extreme circumstances, when a visitor pulls a weapon or injures someone, the Police should be called.

Suspicious Parcel, Briefcase or Bag

In a busy reception area, parcels, briefcases and even plastic bags can be received by, forgotten about or left unattended.

If this happens, the receptionist should attempt to identify who the item belongs to by looking for a name and address that may be attached to the briefcase or written on the parcel. However, under no circumstances should the receptionist attempt to move or open the item in order to identify who it belongs to.

Should the receptionist be unable to safely identify who the item belongs to they should contact security. Security personnel should then make a decision as to whether the building needs to be evacuated and the Police called. If the item begins to smoke or tick before security personnel arrive, the receptionist should set off the fire alarm immediately and telephone the emergency services.

A Visitor Gaining Unauthorised Access to the Main Office

If a receptionist is busy it may be possible for a visitor to make their way into the main office without proper authority. Should this happen, the receptionist should advise security immediately so that they can check CCTV footage in order to identify who has entered the building. While that is being done, security and/or the receptionist will make attempts to identify where the unauthorised visitor is in the building.

Once the unauthorised visitor has been located, security personnel will escort the individual from the premises. If, however, the unauthorised visitor has gained access to confidential information the Police may be phoned in order that the individual is arrested.

In each of the situations above, an Incident/Security Breach Report Form should be completed in order that a record is maintained of what happened and how it was dealt with.

INCIDENT/SECURITY BREACH REPORT FORM	
Name of Person Reporting Incident	John Barr
Position	Receptionist
Date and Time of Incident	25 July 2008
Location that Incident took place	Reception
Description of Incident	Briefcase left unattended in Reception Waiting Area
Action Taken	I checked the briefcase for a name and an address. The name on the briefcase (Mr I Lyons) was the same as a visitor who was in the building for a meeting with Mr Jacks. I contacted Mr Jacks so he could inform his visitor that he had forgotten his briefcase.
Further Action Required	I removed the briefcase from the waiting area and placed it behind my desk until Mr Jacks' secretary came to collect it for the visitor.
Signed	John Barr
Date	July 2008

Questions

1   Tony Bennet, the receptionist at Talbet plc, was unable to deal with the following problems effectively.

◆ Tony could not answer a customer enquiry on the products provided by the organisation.

◆ He was unable to answer a customer enquiry on who was in charge of the Finance Department.

Advise Tony how he could deal with the above situations in future. Give reasons for your answers. (4 PS – G)

2   Suggest two qualities of a good receptionist. Justify your suggestions. (4 KU – C)

Questions continued ➤

?

3   Describe two benefits of using an electronic diary. (2 KU – G)

4   At Dander plc the following problems have recently been identified.

     ◆ The receptionist was unsure which employees were in the building during a recent fire drill.

     ◆ An emergency phone call was received for a Brian Adams. Unfortunately the receptionist was unaware that Brian Adams was visiting one of the managers at the time of the call.

     Suggest one way in which each of these problems could be solved. Give a different solution for each. (2 PS – G)

5   Following a recent review of the reception area the following problems have been identified. Suggest how each of the problems could be overcome. Give a different answer to each.

     ◆ Having signed in, visitors are often left standing in the reception area while waiting to see a manager.

     ◆ A visitor was found in the Finance Department, a restricted area.

     ◆ Homeworkers are often refused entry into the building by the receptionist. (3 PS – G)

6   Jarside plc use CCTV at the main entrance to reception. Suggest and justify two other ways in which security could be improved within the reception area. (4 KU – C)

7   At a recent training event, Jane Parks was asked how she would deal with the following security situations if they occurred at reception.

     ◆ An aggressive visitor.

     ◆ The receptionist fell sick during the day and had to be sent home.

     Suggest how Jane could deal with each of the above problems. Give reasons for your answers. (4 PS – C)

THE WORKING ENVIRONMENT: MAIL HANDLING

Mail

Every day millions of items of mail are sent and received by organisations. The mail that is sent and received can be classified into two main types.

Internal Mail

Internal mail describes mail that is sent within an organisation. In other words, internal mail is mail that is sent between employees in the same organisation. For example:

◆ a memo sent by the Managing Director to all her employees, or

◆ a report sent by one employee to another using email.

External Mail

External mail describes mail that is sent outwith an organisation. In other words, external mail is mail that is sent between the organisation and another party e.g. a customer or another business. For example:

◆ a price list that is sent by the organisation to one of their customers, or

◆ legal documentation that is sent by a solicitor to the organisation.

The Mail Room

Many organisations have a dedicated Mail Room that deals with all the mail that an organisation receives (incoming mail) and sends (outgoing mail). Although, dealing with mail sounds like a fairly straightforward task, a number of different procedures need to be followed in order that it is done successfully.

Dealing with Incoming Mail

Every day the first task that the Mail Room in any organisation will undertake is dealing with any mail that is received by the organisation. The mail received will come from two main sources:

◆ External mail received through the Royal Mail, or a courier service, such as TNT

◆ Internal mail received through its own internal courier service.

As most employees like to deal with any mail received that day before anything else, it is important that the Mail Room deliver each employee's mail before the start of the working day. This means that staff who work in the Mail Room will have to begin their day probably an hour before anybody else so that all mail received can be opened and delivered before other employees arrive for work.

One of the receptionists in an organisation will also have to begin work early as it will be their responsibility to receive the mail from the postman when he arrives. As part of that process, the receptionist may have to sign for any letters that have been sent by special delivery. Any parcels will also be taken by the receptionist before all the mail is then handed to the Mail Room. During the day, the receptionist may receive other items of incoming mail that are delivered by a courier or parcel firm. When such items are received, the receptionist should sign for them before passing them immediately to the Mail Room.

On receiving all the incoming mail, the first thing that the Mail Room staff will do is sort the mail into three main categories:

◆ Private and Personal Mail or Confidential Mail

◆ Urgent Mail

◆ Non-Urgent Mail.

Private and Personal Mail or Confidential Mail

Private and Personal or Confidential mail should not be opened by the Mail Room as the contents are only intended to be read by the person the item is being sent to. Instead, the envelope should be date stamped before being placed in the relevant department tray for delivery.

If the envelope is opened by mistake, it should be immediately re-sealed before writing 'opened in error' across the envelope. The person who opened the item should also sign the envelope.

Urgent Mail

Urgent mail refers to all mail that has been marked urgent on the envelope or has been delivered by a courier. Such mail should always be opened first and delivered without delay to the relevant person.

Non-Urgent Mail

Non-urgent items such as first and second class mail, parcels and internal mail should be opened after the urgent mail has been dealt with. In some instances, items inside such mail will be marked urgent. If they are, they should be delivered to the relevant person without delay.

Handling Urgent and Non-Urgent Mail

Although urgent mail is dealt with before non-urgent mail, both are handled in the same way. First, the contents are removed and then checked to make sure that the enclosures detailed in the letter have been attached. If an item is missing, the Mail Room Assistant should write 'item missing' in pencil at the top of the letter.

All items sent with the letter should then be stapled to the back of the covering letter so that they do not go missing. The covering letter should then be date stamped on a blank part of the letter. Under no circumstances, should cheques or legal documentation be date stamped.

If a cheque is received with a letter, the amount should be checked against the letter before being entered into the Remittances Book. The cheque should then be placed into the Finance Department's tray.

In some instances, letters will be received that need to be seen by more than one person in the organisation. If this is the case, the letter and enclosures should be photocopied. Alternatively, a circulation slip may be attached which lists all the people the letter and enclosures should be passed to.

Once all the actions above have been carried out, the non-urgent mail will be sorted into departments before being distributed to the relevant areas. In some organisations, the non-urgent mail is not delivered in person, but placed in staff or departmental pigeon holes for collection. Urgent mail, of course, is dealt with immediately before being hand delivered to the person the letter is addressed to.

Equipment Used by the Mail Room when Dealing with Incoming Mail

A number of pieces of equipment are used when dealing with incoming mail. These include:

A Letter Opener

Shaped like a knife, but with a narrower blade, a letter opener is used to open an envelope quickly and neatly without damaging the contents within.

Date Stamp

A date stamp is used to stamp items of mail with the date on which they are received by an organisation. Shaped like a hammer head, a date stamp usually has revolving rubber cogs on its face which can be changed according to the date on which the stamp is used.

Stapler

A stapler is used to attach enclosures to a covering letter so that items do not get lost or detached from each other as the mail is being dealt with.

Photocopier

A photocopier is used to make exact copies of correspondence that are to be seen by more than one person in the organisation.

Scanner

A scanner is a device that converts paper-based documents into electronic form. It works to some extent in a similar fashion to a photocopier. In some large organisations all mail, other than personal, private and confidential and catalogues/leaflets, is scanned onto a computer. One of the main reasons for scanning mail onto a computer is that it helps in the move towards a paperless office.

Before mail is scanned, it is sorted into departments and a code added so that each item of mail can be distinguished from all the others. The code added is usually made up of the initials of the department the item is going to and initials of the employee the item is addressed to.

Once the mail has been scanned onto the computer, staff can easily access items that are for them by searching through the scanned items for their departmental and individual codes. Having scanned all the mail, the Mail Room then bundle all the items together and store each day's correspondence in a storage box in case it needs to be referred to at a later date.

By scanning all mail into a computer it is much easier for an employee not only to access current mail, but back-dated correspondence that may relate to the item presently being dealt with. Better yet though, any reply an employee makes to an item of mail can be linked to it by adding the appropriate code when saving the document.

Other benefits of scanning mail are that the Mail Room no longer needs to deliver mail to each department or photocopy items for more than one person to see.

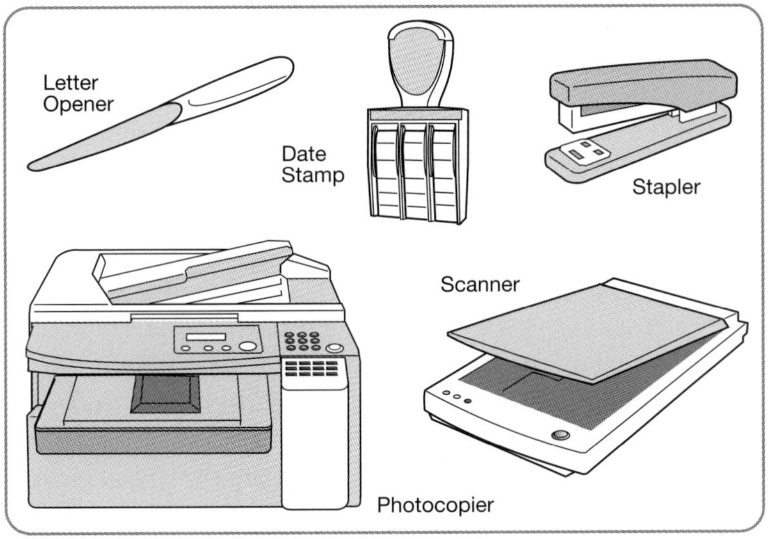

Figure 2.12 An illustration of mail room equipment

Dealing with Outgoing Mail

One of the tasks that a Mail Room will undertake daily is dealing with the mail that an organisation is to send. The outgoing mail that a Mail Room deals with is sent in two main ways:

◆ Externally using the Royal Mail or a courier service, such as Federal Express.

◆ Internally using the organisation's own internal courier service.

As most external mail is sent using the Royal Mail it is important that the Mail Room discover by what time they must deliver the mail to the Post Office for it to be sent that day. There is no point having all the mail organised and franked for the Mail Room Assistant to then arrive at the Post Office and find that it is closed or that the mail for that day has already been collected.

To avoid the above problem, it is important that a Mail Room put in place procedures that allow it to deal with external mail effectively. For example, in some large organisations, a Mail Room Assistant will collect outgoing mail from departments at regular intervals during the day. In other organisations, staff should be advised to take mail to the Mail Room at regular intervals rather than leaving it to the end of the day. Whatever the case, all staff should be advised of what the cut off time is for dealing with items that are to be sent via a Post Office.

When external mail is received by the Mail Room it is sorted into categories: 1st class, 2nd class, Special Delivery, Same Day Delivery (Courier), Parcels and Internal Mail. To assist Mail Room staff, employees should indicate on the top right corner of the envelope how they would like the item sent or place it in the appropriate box in the Mail Room. Before doing this, the person who is sending the letter should check that the correct contents have been placed in the envelope, that the envelope has been sealed and that it has been correctly addressed. In some organisations, this may be the responsibility of Mail Room staff.

1st and 2nd Class Mail

First and Second class mail is dealt with in the same way by the Mail Room. First, the item is checked for size and then it is weighed so that a postal charge can be calculated. Once this has been done, the item is franked and then placed in the appropriate Royal Mail bag that distinguishes 1st from 2nd class mail.

Special Delivery

Special Delivery items require that a form be completed that is then stamped at the Post Office when sent. Part of the form, that contains the sender's name and address, is attached to the back of the envelope. The remaining part of the form is retained by the sender as proof of postage. In order to calculate the postal charge, the Special Delivery item will have to be checked for size and weight before being franked.

Unlike 1st and 2nd class mail, next day delivery is guaranteed by sending an item Special Delivery. The item can also be tracked online which provides the sender with information as to when the item will be delivered. On delivery the individual or organisation receiving the letter must sign for it as evidence of delivery. Should the item being sent be lost, the sender will be entitled to compensation from the Post Office up to a current maximum of £2,500.

Same Day Delivery (Courier)

If an item needs to be delivered immediately a Courier service will be contacted. The Courier will normally collect the item within an hour and then deliver the item as soon as possible thereafter. As with Special Delivery, the item can be tracked online and must be signed for on delivery. The cost of sending an item same day depends upon the Courier used and the item being sent. Unlike other forms of delivery, many Courier services will collect mail at any time of the day and thereafter deliver the item as soon as possible.

Parcels

If necessary, the Mail Room may need to wrap the parcel and then write on the address the item is being sent to. The item should then be checked for size and weight in order that the postal charge can be calculated. Once this has been done, the item can be franked.

Once all the items above have been franked, the mail room supervisor will record the amount of postage used in the Postages Book. The mail room assistant should then take all items that are being sent via the Royal Mail to the Post Office.

Internal Mail

All internal mail should be placed in an internal mail bag which is then collected by the organisation's own courier service. As with external mail being sent through the postal service, there is a cut off time for internal mail. Therefore, it is important that the Mail Room make all staff aware when the internal courier service comes to collect the internal mail bag. It should be noted, however, that in most organisations this is either just before the close of business or just after.

Unlike external mail, internal mail does not need to be checked for weight or size and therefore does not need franked.

Equipment Used by the Mail Room when Dealing with Outgoing Mail

A number of pieces of equipment are used when dealing with outgoing mail. These include:

Big and Small Letter Measure

This device judges whether an item of mail should be priced as a big or a small letter. Basically a plastic board with two rectangular holes cut into it; a big and small letter measure shows the maximum size that a big or small letter can be. Once it is known whether an item is big or small, it can then be weighed to determine how much it will cost to send.

Scales

Scales are used to weigh mail. Once an item has been weighed its postage cost can be calculated by looking in a Royal Mail pricing booklet. Some electronic scales are

HOW TO PASS STANDARD GRADE ADMINISTRATION

able to price mail automatically as the postage costs of differently weighted items have been programmed into the scales. More sophisticated machines are even able to price items which are being sent Special Delivery or overseas.

Franking Machine

A franking machine is used by a Mail Room instead of stamps. Using a dial or a keypad located on the machine, the operator sets the price at which each item of mail will be franked. Each item of mail is then fed through the machine which franks the envelope with the postal charge.

Using such a machine is much quicker than having to lick stamps and avoids the hassle of having to buy stamps. Instead, all the mail room has to do is take part of the machine, called a module, to the Post Office so that it can purchase credit which it then adds to the franking machine. With some franking machines, additional credit can be purchased directly over the phone.

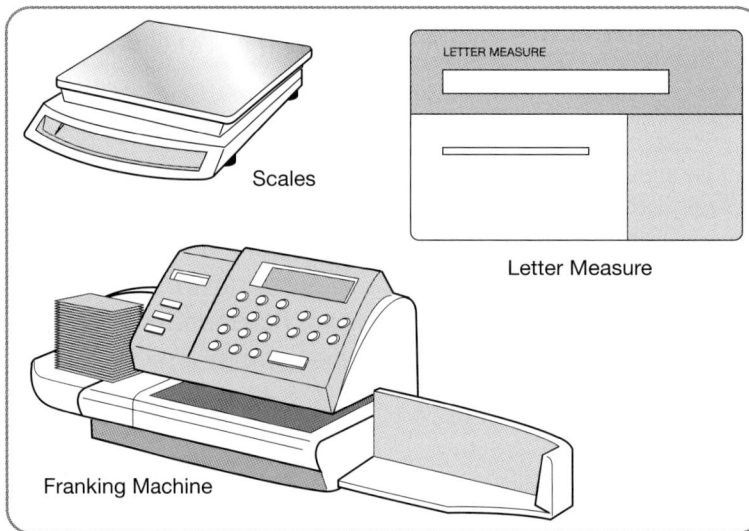

Scales

LETTER MEASURE

Letter Measure

Franking Machine

Figure 2.13 An illustration of more mail room equipment

Alternative Methods of Communicating a Message

On reading the sections above, it may seem that the only way to communicate a message is by sending a letter via the Royal Mail or by using an organisation's own internal courier service. However, in reality there are a number of different ways in which messages can be sent between two people. Some of the most common are noted below:

Memorandum (Memo)

A memo is an internal communication that contains a short message on a specific issue. For example, a memo may be sent by the Sales Director to the Sales Manager informing him of when the next sales meeting is. A memo can also be used to advise staff of internal job vacancies.

The benefits of using a memo to send messages are:

◆ Information written on a memo is usually read by the recipient.

◆ Provides a permanent record of the message sent. Important messages will not be forgotten if sent this way.

◆ The memo can be sent to all staff or attached to the staff notice board. This means all staff will receive the same message.

The drawbacks of using a memo to send messages are:

◆ If sent using the internal courier system it could take 24 hours for the memo to be delivered. This may not be quick enough for urgent messages.

Staff Newsletter

A staff newsletter is a magazine-like document that is given to staff on a monthly basis. It will contain a variety of information relating to the business. Items that may be contained in the newsletter would include: upcoming social events, staff interviews and information on new products.

The benefits of using a staff newsletter to send messages are:

◆ Provides a permanent record of the message sent.

◆ The staff newsletter is sent to all staff which means everyone will receive the same message.

The drawbacks of using a staff newsletter to send messages are:

◆ Some staff just throw away newsletters without reading them.

Public Address System

A public address system is used by organisations, such as Tesco's or Asda, to contact members of staff who are inside the building but always on the move. Throughout the building a number of loudspeakers are used to communicate the message sent over the public address system.

The benefits of using a public address system to send messages are:

◆ Employees can be contacted when they are away from their desk.

◆ The message can be communicated to more than one member of staff at a time.

◆ Messages are communicated to staff quickly.

The drawbacks of using a public address system to send messages are:

◆ Employees may not hear the message if where they are working is noisy.

◆ Everybody hears the message, not just the person it was intended for.

External Courier Service

An external courier service, such as Federal Express, delivers items of mail and parcels in a very similar fashion to the Royal Mail. Items are either taken to the courier's office or picked up by the courier and then delivered to the recipient.

The benefits of using an external courier service to send messages are:

◆ Local deliveries and certain national deliveries can be made on the day.

◆ Overnight delivery is guaranteed for national and some international destinations.

◆ There is proof of delivery. The delivery is signed for when handed to the recipient.

The drawbacks of using an external courier service to send messages are:

◆ Same day delivery or overnight international delivery can be expensive.

Email

Email stands for electronic mail. That is, mail which is sent between two computers that have been linked via a phone line. To operate an email system a user must have an email account and an email address.

The benefits of using email to send messages are:

◆ As emails are transmitted down phone lines, the messages that are sent are received in a matter of seconds.

◆ As phone lines are open 24 hours a day, there is no delay in sending an e-mail.

◆ The same email message can be sent to many people at the same time.

◆ Emails can be sent to anywhere in the world.

◆ Emails can be sent with attachments.

The drawbacks of using email to send messages are:

◆ The information you send must be in electronic form. It is impossible to send a paper-based document using email.

◆ Communicating certain messages by email is seen by many as being inappropriate. For example, a letter firing someone should not be sent by email.

Telephone

A telephone is used to send an oral message down a telephone line to another person. As well as being able to make and receive calls, a modern telephone can receive voicemail messages (see below).

The benefits of using a telephone to send messages are:

◆ It only takes a few seconds to dial a number in order to contact the person you want to speak to.

◆ Telephone calls can be made all around the world.

The drawbacks of using a telephone to send a message are:

◆ An employee may not be there to receive a call because they are out of the office.

◆ International calls can be expensive.

Mobile Phone

A mobile phone is exactly what it says it is – a phone that an employee can carry whilst on the move. As with a traditional telephone, a mobile can make and accept calls as well as receive voicemail messages (see below). In addition, mobile phones are also used to send and receive text messages.

The benefits of using a mobile phone to send messages are:

◆ Employees can be contacted when out of the office on a business trip.

◆ Employees can be contacted 24 hours a day and very quickly.

◆ Mobile phones work all around the world.

The drawbacks of using a mobile phone to send messages are:

◆ Mobile phones only work in areas that have a signal.

◆ International calls can be expensive.

◆ Mobiles should not be used while driving or on an aircraft which means messages can not be sent.

Voicemail

Voicemail is similar to an old-style answering machine. If an employee is unable to answer their telephone, because they are out of the office or in a meeting, the voicemail system will ask the caller to leave a message. On their return to the office, the employee will know a message has been left because either the phone will have a light on it which is flashing or the dialling tone will be different. To pick up the message that has been left, the employee dials their voicemail box and then types in their pin code.

The benefits of using voicemail to send messages are:

◆ A message can be left at anytime during the day.

◆ Messages can be picked up at anytime during the day.

◆ It avoids the problem of another employee having taken a message forgetting to pass it on or passing it on wrongly.

The drawbacks of using voicemail to send messages are:

◆ The message may not be picked up if the employee does not check their voicemail regularly.

◆ It can be difficult to leave a clear and concise voicemail message that will be understood.

Pager

A pager is an electronic device about half the size of a mobile phone that can be attached to a belt or a part of clothing. It is used to contact employees while they are out of the office. If an employee needs to be contacted, the organisation sends a message to the employee's pager. When the message arrives, the pager will ring letting the employee know they have to contact the office. On some more advanced pagers, a message and a contact telephone number are displayed.

The benefits of using a pager to send messages are:

◆ Employees can be contacted when out of the office on a business trip.

◆ Employees can be contacted 24 hours a day and in a matter of seconds.

◆ Sending a pager message is inexpensive.

The drawbacks of sending a pager message are:

◆ Pagers only work in areas that have a signal.

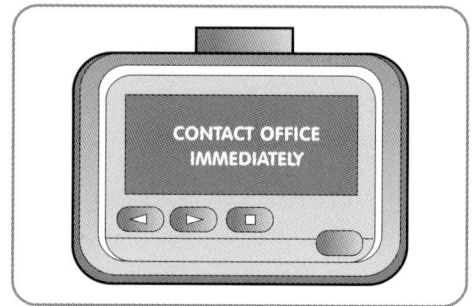

Figure 2.14 An illustration of a pager

Fax

A fax machine is a digital device that allows paper-based documents that contain text, graphics or photographs to be sent down a telephone line. At the other end, the receiving fax machine produces an exact copy of the document that was sent.

The benefits of using a fax to send messages are:

◆ It takes only a short period of time to send a fax.

◆ A fax message can be sent anywhere in the world to another fax machine.

◆ Faxes can be sent at anytime as telephone lines are open 24 hours a day.

◆ Paper-based documents can be sent digitally very quickly.

The drawbacks of using a fax to send messages are:

◆ Faxes usually only accept documents that are A4 or smaller.

◆ A separate telephone line is needed for sending and receiving faxes.

Figure 2.15 An illustration of a fax

Intranet

An intranet is a form of computer network that operates within an organisation. Information that is held on an organisation's intranet is not available to people outside the business. All employees in the organisation are able to access the intranet and the information stored on it. In most organisations the information contained on an intranet is in the same format as your would find on the internet.

The benefits of using an intranet to communicate a message are:

◆ Notice board areas can be set up on the intranet site to let employees know about new job vacancies or new health and safety procedures in the organisation.

◆ All memos and reports can be displayed on the intranet meaning time and money will be saved printing and delivering a copy to each employee.

The drawbacks of using an intranet to communicate a message are:

◆ Some employees may not look at the organisation's intranet site on a regular basis meaning they miss out on important information.

Internet

The internet is a communications network that links computers all over the world. This is done through a number of powerful servers that are located throughout the world. These servers store the information that anyone can access when on the internet.

The benefits of using the internet to communicate a message are:

◆ An organisation can put messages on its internet site about new products, upcoming events and special promotions. Anyone who enters the organisation's site will have instant access to this information.

◆ It is cheap and fairly straightforward to add information to a web site.

The drawbacks of using the internet to communicate a message are:

◆ An internet site is only useful if people use it.

Choosing the most Appropriate Method to Communicate a Message

Deciding which method of communication to use when sending a message is very important. This is because, if the wrong method is used the message being sent may arrive too late or come across in the wrong way. It is therefore vital that the most appropriate method is used.

Many pupils struggle when asked to justify an answer. When justifying it is important to explain why you have chosen a certain method. See the next page for examples.

Example

Problem: A catalogue needs to arrive at the printers by 4p.m. today so that a print run can begin.

Method: External Courier Service

Justification: The catalogue needs to be at the printers today. An external courier service will pick the catalogue up from the office and then guarantee same day delivery to the printers.

Problem: A customer has called to change the location of a meeting. Unfortunately the manager has already left for the meeting and is unaware of the change.

Method: Mobile telephone and voicemail

Justification: The manager needs to know of the change straight way. If they are unable to answer their mobile, leave a message on their voicemail so that they pick up the message at the earliest opportunity.

Problem: Invitations need to be sent to a number of customers asking them to a gala day in 2 months time.

Method: Second class mail

Justification: The invitations are not urgent. Sending a letter also looks professional. Sending the letter second class will keep costs lower.

Problem: A word processed report is required at Head Office in London immediately.

Method: Email

Justification: The report needs to arrive quickly. Emails can be sent with attachments. If the report is confidential, the email may have to be password protected.

Problem: Betty Franks is required to man the reception desk while the receptionist takes a break. Unfortunately, Betty is away from her desk and no one knows where she is in the building.

Method: Public Address System

Justification: As the public address system is wired throughout the building the message will get to Betty quickly wherever she is. It does not matter if the message is sent using the public address system as it is not confidential.

Example continued ➤

Example *continued*

Problem: Legal documents received by a local branch need to be sent to the organisation's legal department.

Method: Internal courier service

Justification: Using the organisation's own internal courier service is safe and secure. It is unlikely the legal documents will get lost. The legal documents will arrive the next day.

Problem: A letter needs to be sent to a customer informing them that legal action is to be taken against them for non-payment of a bill.

Method: Special Delivery

Justification: It is important that the customer receives the letter. By sending it special delivery the organisation will have proof of delivery as the customer will have to sign for the letter. Sending an item special delivery also lets the customer know that the issue is important.

Problem: Employees need to be advised of internal job vacancies.

Method: Intranet and internal memo placed on staff notice board

Justification: All staff have access to the intranet via the organisation's network and can easily check what vacancies are available. If the vacancies are placed on the staff notice board it will be easy and convenient for staff to check them.

Problem: A customer has requested directions for a meeting they have with a manager at your office tomorrow.

Method: Fax

Justification: The customer needs the information fairly quickly. A straightforward map with directions can be drawn onto a piece of paper and then faxed to the customer.

Questions

1 Explain what role a receptionist may have in dealing with incoming mail. (2 KU – G)

2 After a recent review of mail handling procedures the following problem was identified.

◆ Staff are not receiving incoming mail until an hour after they start work.

How could the above problem be solved? (1 PS – G)

3 Explain what is meant by the term external mail. (1 KU – G)

4 Name and describe two pieces of equipment which may be used by staff when dealing with incoming mail. (4 KU – G)

5 John Barr, the Mail Room Supervisor, has received the following complaints:

◆ A number of urgent letters have missed the postal collection.

◆ A number of letters have been returned by the Post Office as they are incorrectly priced.

How could the above problems be solved? (2 PS – G)

6 Name and describe two pieces of equipment which Mail Room staff may use when dealing with outgoing mail. (4 KU – G)

7 The following problems have arisen today at Younis Ltd. Suggest and justify an appropriate method of communication that should be used to send each message.

◆ A number of internal job vacancies have been created which staff need to be made aware of.

◆ Advising a number of job candidates that they have been invited to an interview in 2 weeks time.

◆ A new health and safety procedure is to be introduced. All departmental managers need to be made aware of the procedure.

◆ An urgent purchase order needs to be received by a supplier within the next 20 minutes for it to be processed today.

You should use a different method each time. (8 PS – C)

8 Suggest and justify two methods of sending letters and/or parcels. (4 KU – C)

STORAGE AND RETRIEVAL OF INFORMATION: PURPOSE OF FILING

Although filing is probably one of the most boring tasks that an administration assistant will have to do, it is also one of the most important. Being able to find files quickly and easily is vital if an organisation is to operate effectively. This is because files contain important information that managers will use to help them make decisions.

A Good Filing System

The key to a good filing system is that documents should be easy and quick to locate. To achieve this, the organisation should use a straightforward filing method that makes it easy to keep documents in the correct order. Filing cabinets should also be located as close to the main office as possible so that those who need to access them can do so easily.

It is also important that all files are kept safe and secure. This means that all files should be stored in lockable cabinets that are fire and water proof. In the case of confidential information, a separate cabinet may be used that only authorised members of staff have access to.

Within each cabinet, individual files should be protected from wear and tear by placing them in folders or plastic wallets. To improve this situation, there should be enough cabinets so that files do not need to be crammed together.

As the number of files is likely to grow in size over time it is important that the area where the filing cabinets are stored has enough space for new cabinets to be added. It should also be fairly straightforward to move files from one cabinet to another.

Finally, the filing system should be cost effective to set up. It should not take up too much space and it should be fairly inexpensive to maintain.

Maintaining a Good Filing System

It is all very well creating a good filing system, but if it is not maintained properly it will soon become useless.

One of the major problems that filing systems can suffer from is documents not being filed. All too often employees will remove files but then fail to return them to the filing cabinet when finished looking at the information. Instead, files are placed in a huge pile beside the filing cabinets. This situation becomes even worse when new files are created, but no one takes the time to file them in a cabinet. In the end, the organisation is left with lots of un-filed documents that become difficult to locate, or worse still, lost.

To avoid the above situation, an administration assistant should be made responsible for filing all documents and making sure they are kept in the correct order. Of course, to help the administration assistant it is important that documents that are ready for filing are marked in some way. In some instances this will involve placing an 'F' in the top right corner of the document, placing a diagonal line through the document, or stamping 'For File' on it.

Once the administration assistant has identified what documents are for filing they should then put the documents into alphabetical order. By doing this documents that are meant to go into the same file can be identified. At the same time, any documents that need to be kept together should be stapled. Paper clips should not be used as they can come off or attach to other documents.

Having got the documents in order, the administrative assistant should then place them into the appropriate files in date order, the most recent document going at the front of the file. To assist the administrative assistant and so speed up the filing process, many organisations ask employees to place 'out guides' or 'absent markers' in the location from which they removed a file. By doing this, it makes it a lot easier for the administration assistant to file the item correctly when it is returned. It also saves other employees searching around for a file that has already been removed.

As well as ensuring all files are filed correctly, an organisation must also make sure that each file is maintained properly. For example, if confidential or valuable information is stored separately, cross references should be used. On the front cover of the main file a cross reference should be made to the confidential information so that whoever is looking at the file is aware that other information exists.

As well as cross referencing, it is important that old documents are removed at regular intervals so that files do not become overloaded with outdated information. However, this must be done carefully as some documents, such as legal documentation or bank records, must be held for a certain period of time by law. Any old documents which are removed should be properly disposed of using a shredder. Under no circumstances should old documents be disposed of in a bin.

Finally, at the end of the day, all files should be securely locked inside a fire and waterproof cabinet in order to protect them.

Questions

1 Lonpop Ltd have identified the following problems with their filing procedures.

- ◆ Out of date documents which contain customers' personal details were discovered dumped in bins.

- ◆ A number of searches have been initiated for lost files only to find out later that a member of staff already had the file out.

- ◆ Staff have complained that a number of files contain material which should not have been filed.

Suggest and justify how each of the above problems could be avoided in the future. (3 PS – C)

STORAGE AND RETRIEVAL OF INFORMATION: METHODS

i It is all very well deciding to set up a filing system, but if the files are not kept in an order the system is little better than useless. There are three main methods that can be used to put files in order.

Hints and Tips

Make sure you know the advantages and disadvantages of each manual filing system. Pupils often struggle with this type of question in the written exam.

Alphabetical

With this system all files are arranged in alphabetical order. Generally, the customer's surname is used to decide what letter of the alphabet they should be placed under. In the case of a business, the first letter of the business name is used.

To make it easy to find where each letter starts, guide cards or tabs are used. In the case of popular letters such as M, there may be a subdivision such as Ma, Mc and Mo.

Advantages

◆ An alphabetical filing system is easy to use and understand. As long as you know the alphabet and the name of the customer you are looking for, it is fairly straightforward to locate and file documents.

◆ Such a filing system is also easy to set up as all you need is knowledge of the alphabet and enough filing cabinets to put the files in.

◆ As the system is so easy to use and set up it is popular with small- to medium-sized organisations that do not have too many customers.

Disadvantages

◆ Although filing files alphabetically sounds easy, in reality it requires a good knowledge of filing rules. For example, "The Red Cross" would be filed under 'R', rather than 'T'.

◆ It is also the case that if a lot of customers have the same surname e.g. Smith, it can take a while to find a particular customer's file.

◆ An alphabetical filing system is not suitable for organisations which are growing in size and have lots of new customers. As the business grows, more filing cabinets will be required to store the new customers' files. To ensure the alphabetical system remains tidy and in order, files will have to be continually moved to new cabinets so that there is enough space. This is time consuming and laborious.

Numerical

All files are arranged in number order. Any new file is just given the next number in the sequence and then added to the filing cabinet. For example, if the last file was 10045, the next file would be given the number 10046.

Advantages

◆ Such a system tends to be used by large organisations that have lots of customers who have the same surname. As long as the customer remembers their file number, the problem of finding a customer's file when they have the same surname as other customers is eliminated. Many organisations assist their customers in remembering their file numbers by quoting it as the reference on all correspondence they send. By doing this, a customer can easily quote their file number when phoning the organisation.

◆ As files are in number order it is fairly easy to understand the system and thus file files correctly.

◆ Unlike an alphabetical system, a numerical system can be easily expanded without a massive reorganisation of the existing files. New files are just added to the end of the current files, rather than throughout, as is the case with an alphabetical system.

Disadvantages

◆ A numerical system usually needs to be supported by an alphabetical system. This is because customers often forget what their numerical file number is which makes it very difficult to identify their file. To overcome this problem, organisations create an alphabetical index which matches each customer's surname to their numerical file number. This alphabetical list requires to be continually updated as new customer files are created and old ones deleted.

◆ Unlike an alphabetical system, where correspondence from customers who do not write regularly can be placed at the start of each letter, a numerical system finds it hard to deal with such correspondence.

Chronological

All files are arranged in chronological (date order). This system does not tend to be used as a primary method of filing but rather to support other methods. For example, if filing alphabetically, all documents within a particular file will be filed in date order.

Advantages

◆ When looking through a file it is easy to see how a customer has progressed over a period of time. For example, looking at a pupil's record over their first 4 years at secondary school will show how they have progressed in each subject.

◆ This can be the most suitable way of storing back dated information that is no longer kept in an organisation's main files. For example, the files of pupils who have left a school may be stored according to the year they left.

Disadvantages

◆ If an organisation were to use it as its only method of filing it would be nearly impossible to locate a customer's file as different parts of the file would be in several places under different dates. It would therefore be impossible to remember where each part was.

◆ Even if an alphabetical index was used to match each customer's surname to different dates it would take a long time to locate a customer's file.

Storing Files Electronically – File Management

With an electronic (computerised) storage system all files are stored on a computer's hard drive, a network's server or a CD-ROM. Even if a document is in paper form it can be scanned into the computer and then saved. All saved documents are then kept in order by placing them in folders on a computer's hard drive. This is called file management.

Good file management is about saving documents using appropriate names that make sense and which will be easy to find at a later date. In order to assist this process, documents should be saved into what are known as folders. These are areas where documents that are connected in some way are stored together. For example, all Administration documents would be stored in an Administration folder. However, as there are likely to be lots of Administration documents, sub folders will be created inside the main Administration folder. Sub folders called Standard Grade, Intermediate 2 and Higher may be created into which appropriate documents should be saved.

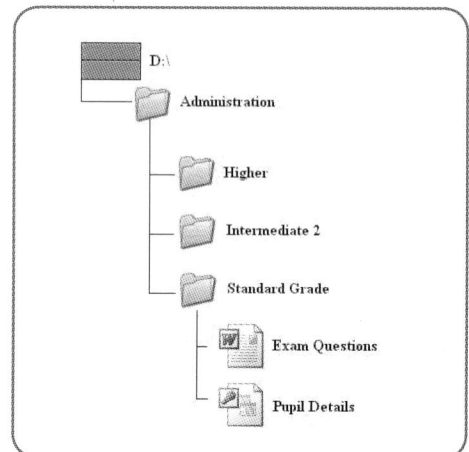

Figure 3.1 An illustration of good file management

As well as allowing folders to be created into which saved documents can be placed, an electronic file management system makes it easy to delete old files that are no longer needed, copy files so they can be placed in more than one folder, rename and move files so that they are easy to find.

Comparison of Manual versus Electronic Storage

Storage Space Required

A manual storage system uses bulky filing cabinets to store documents, whereas an electronic system only requires a computer's hard drive. If additional files are required to be stored, extra filing cabinets may need to be purchased which can be expensive. A computer's hard drive, on the other hand, has space for millions of files meaning extra files can be saved easily and cheaply at no extra cost.

In some organisations, paper-based documents are recorded onto microfilm which reduces an A4 piece of paper to approximately the size of a finger nail. The microfilm is stored in rolls or as microfiche, a sheet of film which can hold hundreds of A4 size documents. By using microfilm the space required to store paper-based documents is greatly reduced.

Locating and Accessing Documents

In a manual storage system documents have to be located by personally looking through filing cabinets or different sheets of microfiche. If the files and microfiche are maintained in a good order then this is fairly easy. However, if they are not, the process can be very difficult.

With an electronic storage system, searches can be used to find files quickly. However, if files are saved using poor file names or are placed in incorrect folders then they can be difficult to find.

As all files are stored on a computer when using electronic storage, documents can be accessed from wherever there is a computer. However, with a manual storage system, an employee will have to go to the room where the filing cabinets are stored to access documents. If documents have been stored on microfiche, the employee will have to feed the film into a reader in order to view and access the information required. Although this is fairly straightforward, it can take time to locate information on microfiche.

Although, it is easier to access electronic files, many employees prefer to read paper-based files that are stored manually. This is because they can handle them and move them about to show other people.

Security
Fire and flood proof filing cabinets are usually used to store files which keeps them safe. Confidential documents can be stored in a separate lockable filing cabinet that can only be opened by an authorised employee.

An electronic storage system can use passwords to prevent unauthorised people accessing certain files. At regular intervals all files on an electronic system are backed up onto tapes or CD-ROMs.

If the system fails because a virus attacks the computer or some files are deleted by mistake, the back up files stored on tapes and CDs can be used to restore everything that has been lost. Unfortunately, a manual system has no such back up unless files have been recorded onto microfilm. If, however, microfilming has not been used, original documents cannot be replaced if lost or destroyed.

Using and Maintaining the System
As a manual storage is fairly easy to understand and use, employees require very little training in how to use it. With an electronic system, employees normally require training in how to use the system effectively.

If training is not given, many employees will use an electronic system poorly. Files will be saved incorrectly and in inappropriate folders meaning they will be harder to find. If a lot of employees do this, it will be difficult to keep an electronic system in order.

However, if training is given, employees can take advantage of the additional options such a system offers. For example, files can be copied, deleted, moved and renamed very easily using an electronic file management system. This is much harder to do and more time consuming when using a manual system.

Storing Files Electronically
Digital information can be stored in many different ways. The most common way is on a computer's hard drive which stores the software applications loaded onto your computer along with any files created and saved using those applications. As a hard drive has Random Access Memory (RAM), files that have been

saved can be recalled, altered and then saved again. Most hard drives have a storage capacity around about 100 GB.

Historically, files have also been saved onto floppy disks. However, as their storage capacity is limited to 1.44 MB they have increasingly become redundant as they do not have enough storage space to hold some files. Nevertheless, many computers still have floppy disk drives and as the disks are so inexpensive to purchase many people still use them to back up data, or to transfer documents between computers.

The next step up from a floppy disk is a zip disk. As with floppy disks, zip disks require a special drive to save data to and from the computer's hard drive. Although zip disks can store between 100–250 MB of information they have become less popular as new more powerful forms of digital storage have come onto the market.

One of the most commonly used storage devices at present is compact discs (CD) which have a storage capacity of 650 MB. As so much information can be stored on a CD it is possible to store reference material from newspapers and encyclopaedias on them.

In order to view the information on a CD a computer must have a CD drive. Although it is fairly easy to view and transfer data held on a CD onto a computer's hard drive, it is not so easy transferring data from a hard drive onto a CD unless the computer has a CD burner software application installed.

A USB (Universal Serial Bus) Flash Drive (also known as a pen drive) is another popular form of electronic storage device which has a capacity of between 60 MB and 4 GB. Unlike a CD, a USB Flash Drive does not need special software to transfer data to and from a hard drive. Due to this, and their portability and the speed at which files can be transferred, this type of storage device is becoming increasingly popular.

Another form of storage which is mainly used for storing film and video are DVDs (Digital Versatile Disc). DVDs have a storage capacity between 4.7 and 17 GB. As with CDs, a DVD burner software application must be installed to transfer data from a computer's hard drive onto a DVD.

Questions

?

1 Rest Rite Ltd want to create a manual filing system for storing their customers' records. Suggest an appropriate manual filing system that Rest Rite Ltd could use. Justify your recommendation. (3 PS – C)

2 The only way to back up paper-based documents is by photocopying them. Explain why this statement is incorrect. (2 KU – C)

3 Describe two features of an effective electronic file management system. (2 KU – G)

4 Trojan Horse Ltd has transferred all its records from a manual to an electronic storage system. The following concerns have been raised.

◆ Staff are finding it difficult to locate records as all files have been lumped together on the system.

◆ A member of staff wants to work on a large database file at home, but it is too big to email.

Provide a different solution to each of the above problems. (2 PS – G)

STORAGE AND RETRIEVAL OF INFORMATION: SECURITY OF INFORMATION

Storing and Using Digital/Electronic Information Safely and Securely

Storing information digitally on computer hard drives, floppy disks, CDs, flash drives and DVDs has many benefits. Nevertheless, if an organisation stores the information in an unsafe environment or does not keep it secure, it can easily become corrupted, lost or destroyed. Similarly, if the digital information is accessed in an irresponsible manner it can quite easily cause a computer to crash with the result that information will be lost.

Storing and Using Digital Information Safely

As a rule, digital information should never be stored or placed close to a magnetic source as this will wipe any information held. It is also important that digital information is not exposed to extreme temperatures, be they hot or cold, as this can cause the information to be destroyed. Water can also affect digital information if spilt onto it or immersed in it. For example, spilling water onto a hard drive will cause it to short circuit making it very difficult to access the information held on it.

Specific measures employed to ensure digital information is stored and used safely include:

Labelling
All floppy disks, CDs and DVDs should be accurately labelled so that employees know what is on them. To prevent CDs or DVDs being scratched, the labels should be written on before being attached.

Disk Boxes and Plastic Wallets
Using disk boxes and plastic wallets prevents floppy disks, CDs and DVDs from getting scratched if left on a desk.

Use According to Instructions
Floppy disks should never be forced into the disk drive as this can rip off the metal casing protecting the information.

Floppy Disks, CDs, DVDs and Flash drives should never be removed from a computer while digital information is still being transferred. Usually an information box on the computer screen or the disk drive light flashing off will indicate that the transfer is complete.

The hard drive of a computer should not be turned off until all programs and files have been closed. Shutting down a computer's hard drive before this has been done could cause information to be lost or corrupted.

Storing and Using Digital Information Securely

Storing and using digital information securely is one of the most important issues that an organisation needs to address. In fact, by law, all organisations that hold information digitally are obliged to make sure that it is stored securely and can not be accessed by unauthorised personnel.

Specific measures employed to ensure digital information is stored and used securely include:

Security Marking

Hard drives can be security marked using an invisible ink permanent marker. If a hard drive is stolen, and then found by the Police they can identify who it belongs to by using a spray which highlights the invisible ink marking.

Lockable Cabinets and Boxes

At the end of the day, digital information that is stored on floppy disks, CDs, DVDs and flash drives should either be placed in a lockable box or cabinet in order to prevent theft.

Locked Rooms

In large organisations, servers that store information and programs will be located in rooms which can only be accessed with a key, swipe card or through typing in a keypad entry code.

Passwords

In order to protect information held on computers most organisations use passwords to prevent or restrict access to all or certain files. In most cases a password will have to be entered along with a username before an employee can log on and then access files.

Passwords are usually made up of a mixture of numbers and letters. The password that an employee chooses should be something that can be easily remembered, but not easily guessed by someone else. It should not be the employee's date of birth or a pet's name, rather a mixture of letters and numbers which are in upper and lower case.

Under no circumstances should an employee write their password down or tell someone else what it is. If an employee thinks someone knows their password they should alter it immediately and report the incident to their line manager.

Swipecards or Keycards

Some organisations require that a keycard or a swipecard be swiped across a reader before an employee can access certain information.

Such systems are put in place not only to restrict access to certain files, but also so an employee has to seek authorisation from a supervisor before they can carry out a task. Only once the supervisor has swiped their card and entered their password will the employee be able to complete their task.

Similar security measures used to restrict access to information include voiceprint, fingerprint and iris recognition as well as signature scanners.

Organisational Procedures

Public Areas

If an employee needs to leave their computer unattended, even for a short period of time, it is important that a password protected screensaver is activated. This is especially the case if the computer is in an area that the general public have access to. If a password protect screensaver is not available, the computer should be shut down so that nobody can access the information.

In public areas, all disks and CDs should be removed from drives and locked in a cabinet or a drawer if an employee needs to leave their desk. While at their desk, an employee should position their screen so that the general public can not read what is on it.

Backing Up Data

Although using a password to protect files stored on a computer system is an effective way of keeping data secure it is not foolproof. For example, a computer system may develop a fault which means data is lost, or there may be a flood or fire which results in the system being destroyed.

In order to guard against the above circumstances, an organisation should make an exact copy of all the information it holds on its computer system at regular intervals. This process is called backing up.

Ideally organisations should back up their computer system at least once a day onto tapes or disks. These back ups should then be stored in a secure area, which is different to where the computer system is located e.g. a separate building or cabinet.

Should a problem occur and data is lost, the back up tapes can be used to re-store any information destroyed.

Anti-Virus Software

One of the major threats to storing digital information safely is viruses. Viruses are software programs that interfere with the normal running of a computer system. Although some viruses just display a funny message on a screen, others infect a computer's hard drive and wipe all the information from it. Some even lie in the computer's hard drive in order to spy on any transactions that are being carried out so that access to confidential information can be obtained.

Viruses are particularly dangerous because they can be spread using email. If an infected email is opened it allows the virus into the computer system. This is why many organisations tell their employees to delete suspicious emails. Once a virus is in a system it can be very costly to repair any damage done. To prevent this it is important to install anti-virus software which prevents such viruses infiltrating an organisation's computer system and deletes suspicious emails before they arrive in employees' inboxes. Anti-virus software also scans for viruses that are already in the computer system so that they can be eliminated.

In order that a computer system is protected from new threats, an organisation should regularly update its anti-virus software.

Data Protection Acts

The Data Protection Acts (1984 and 1998) govern the way in which information is gathered, stored and used. While the 1984 Act only covered information held on computer systems, the 1998 Act applies to certain manually held information such as school and health records.

Under the legislation, any organisation that holds information about living people must be registered as a data user with the Data Protection Registrar. As a data user, an organisation will be responsible for meeting certain provisions. These provisions include: i) that the information is collected and processed lawfully, ii) that the organisation only collects and holds information that it is authorised by the Data Protection Registrar to do so, iii) that information collected is only used in a way that has been authorised by the Data Protection Registrar, iv) that information is only provided to other organisations if authorised by the Data Protection Registrar, v) that information collected is accurate and

kept up to date, vi) that only information needed by the organisation is collected (it should not be excessive or irrelevant), vii) that information is held securely; and viii) that information is held for only as long as it is needed.

Under the Acts, provisions have also been made to give individuals certain rights over the information that is held about them. These include: i) individuals are allowed to access information that is held about them, and ii) individuals can have incorrect information that is held about them amended, corrected or erased.

If the above provisions are not met the Data Protection Registrar can do one of three things: i) serve an enforcement notice, which informs an organisation they must follow certain action in order to correct information they hold, ii) serve a deregistration notice which cancels part or whole of an organisation's right to collect, process and hold information, and iii) serve a transfer prohibition notice which prevents an organisation transferring the data overseas.

Hints and Tips

Make sure you know what the main provisions of the Data Protection Act are. It is a common exam question that is often answered poorly.

Questions

1   Nano plc has recently converted from a manual filing system to a computerised system. The following problems have been identified.

◆ Confidential files can be accessed by any member of staff.

◆ Sensitive information has been left on computer screens by members of staff when they go for their lunch.

◆ A virus from an email has infected the system.

Suggest and justify how the above problems may be overcome. (6 PS – C)

2   Describe two provisions of the Data Protection Act. (2 KU – G)

3   Explain what is meant by the term 'backing-up'. (1 KU – G)

4   Suggest one reason why 'backing-up' electronic files is important. (1 KU – G)

Chapter 4

REPROGRAPHICS

The main task undertaken by the reprographics section in an organisation is the photocopying of documents and papers. As well as photocopying, reprographics will be responsible for finishing the copied documents as requested. For example, the photocopied document may have to be stapled, punched, laminated or bound. In order to carry out these tasks successfully, a number of pieces of equipment are required.

Reprographics Equipment

Photocopier

This is the most important piece of equipment used in the reprographics section. Put simply, a photocopier is a machine which allows an exact copy of a document to be made from one piece of paper to another.

As well as being able to produce exact copies, photocopiers have a number of other features, which assist a reprographics assistant when carrying out their duties. These include: i) being able to enlarge an A4 document onto A3 paper or even shrink it onto A5 paper, ii) having a feeder which allows multi-page documents to be fed into the photocopier automatically, iii) being able to collect in order the pages of a multi-page document that is being copied several times at once (this is called collation), iv) being able to automatically staple documents while being photocopied, v) being able to copy in colour, vi) being able to copy onto Overhead Projector (OHP) transparencies, and vii) being able to copy directly from a computer.

Laminator

A laminator is a piece of equipment which coats paper or card in a thin film of clear plastic. By coating the document in a protective plastic coating it becomes a lot more durable. Stains can easily be wiped from the plastic and the document does not become torn if handled regularly.

Laminators are used to protect health and safety or fire notices which are placed around a building. Staff ID badges are also usually laminated in order to make them more durable. Pages from a manual can also be laminated, especially if the manual is located in an area of the building where it could easily get dirty or wet.

Binder

A binder is a piece of equipment which allows a multi-page document to be fastened together using a plastic binder. By binding a document together it is less likely that pages will come loose and be lost. This is because a plastic binder fastens a document at several points which gives strength to it.

Documents that tend to be bound include reports, manuals or instruction booklets. Not all documents are bound as stapling is a lot cheaper and quicker to do than binding.

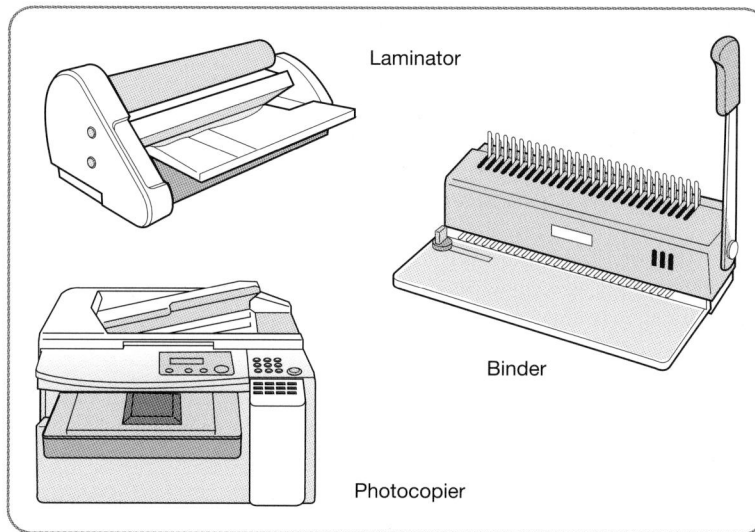

Figure 4.1 Reprographics equipment

Scanner

A scanner is an electronic device which uses a light-sensitive scanning device to convert paper-based documents into a digital form. Once converted, the documents can then be saved as computer files.

Organisations can use scanners to scan all incoming mail, or simply just to convert certain paper-based documents into a digital format so that they can be stored or emailed.

Hole Punch

A hole punch is a piece of equipment which makes holes in a paper document so that it can be placed in a ring binder. In some organisations, a drill-like device will be used to make holes in multi-page documents which a traditional hole punch could not.

Staple Gun

Some reprographics departments have powerful staple guns which can staple multi-page documents which a traditional stapler could not.

Desk Top Publishing (DTP) Software

In some organisations, the reprographics section will be responsible for producing magazines, booklets, newsletters, catalogues, posters and other such documents. To be successful in this task, Desk Top Publishing (DTP) software, such as Microsoft Publisher, will have to be used.

This software allows a reprographics assistant to bring together text, graphics and photographs in one document ready for publishing. Using the software, a reprographics assistant can move, format and manipulate items on a page so that a high-quality publication is produced.

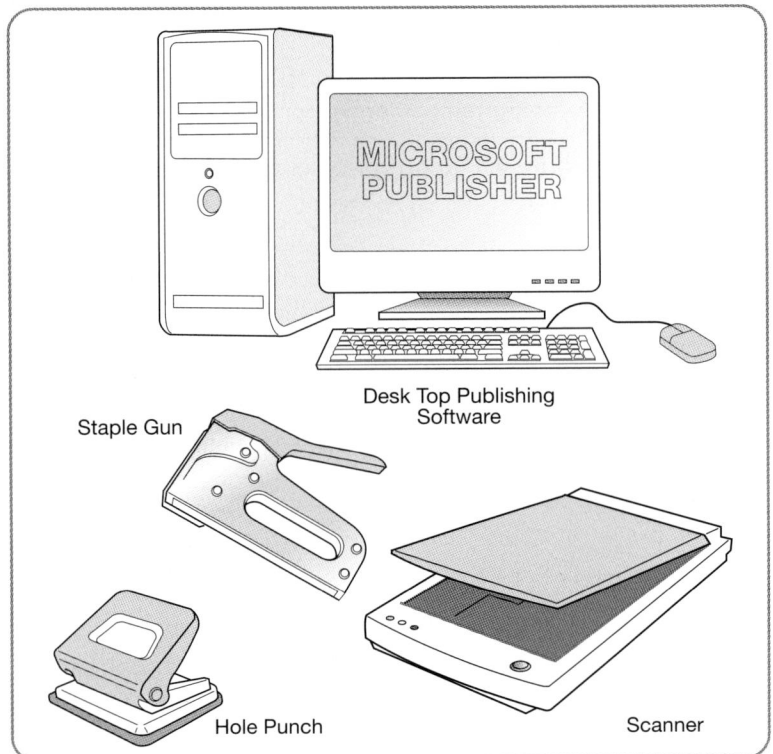

MICROSOFT PUBLISHER

Desk Top Publishing Software

Staple Gun

Hole Punch

Scanner

Figure 4.2 Reprographics equipment

Training Staff to Use Reprographics Equipment

Training staff in the use of reprographics equipment is important for two main reasons: i) to use reprographics equipment effectively an employee will have to be aware of all the features that the equipment offers, and ii) reprographics equipment can be dangerous if used inappropriately.

During the training process, the reprographics assistant should be shown exactly how to use the equipment by a trained and qualified member of staff. The training should be practical and demonstrate how all the functions of the equipment are used safely. Having demonstrated how the equipment is used, the trainer should watch as the employee practises using the equipment.

Although all employees should be given basic training, only those that work in the reprographics section or who are responsible for maintaining the equipment require specialist training. Whatever the case, the training should not just be a one off, but be available at regular intervals so that employees can refresh their skills.

When a new item of equipment is purchased it is important that the reprographics assistant is trained in its use before being allowed to use it. If not, the equipment may be used incorrectly which may break it, or worse still, cause an accident.

As well as being trained in the use of the equipment, the reprographics assistant should also be shown what to do if the item breaks down or a fault arises. For example, if a photocopier starts to smoke, the reprographics assistant should be told to: i) switch the item off, ii) attach an 'out-of-order' sign to the photocopier, iii) call a qualified engineer to repair it, iv) complete a Hazard Report Form, and v) under no circumstances should they try to repair it.

The training given should also make reprographics staff aware of the law relating to the photocopying of items which are copyright protected. For example, all books are copyright protected and can not legally be photocopied unless the author has given their permission.

Reprographics staff should also be advised of organisational procedures for photocopying. For example, in some organisations only some managers have the authority to have items copied.

Staff should also be shown the organisation's photocopying request form and informed how to use it correctly. If staff do not know which parts of the form to complete in order to get certain things done, their photocopying will be completed incorrectly and wastage will occur. At the same time, all staff should be made aware of all the facilities that the reprographics section offers e.g. binding, laminating.

HOW TO PASS STANDARD GRADE ADMINISTRATION

In-House versus External Agency Copying

When photocopying is undertaken within an organisation it is referred to as In-House copying. However, if the photocopying is outsourced to an agency that is not part of the organisation this is called Outside or External Agency copying.

The factors that will influence whether copying occurs In-House or at an External Agency include:

Photocopier Available

If an organisation has an industrial-sized photocopier then a substantial amount of In-House copying will occur. However, if only a small photocopier is owned an External Agency may be used for large amounts of photocopying.

Cost

Using an External Agency can be costly compared with copying the item using In-House facilities.

Special Requirements

In some instances the document to be copied has special requirements. For example, a catalogue may have to be copied onto glossy paper and in colour. It may be the case that this type of copying can only be undertaken by an External Agency.

Location of External Agency

If the External Agency is located a considerable distance from the organisation it may not be worthwhile using it as it would take too long to get the photocopied items back.

Quality Required

As an External Agency has all the best facilities and highly trained employees it is likely that they will be able to produce better quality photocopies than if done In House. For example, an External Agency will have access to superior binding facilities which will make multi-page documents look more professional than if stapled.

Quantity Required

If a document needs to be copied thousands of times an External Agency may be used as it will have many industrial-sized photocopiers that can produce thousands of copies very quickly. Even if an organisation has an industrial-sized photocopier it may use an External Agency so that its own copier does not get clogged up with one job for a long period of time.

Hints *and* **Tips**

Make sure you know the differences between In-House and External Agency photocopying. It is a common exam question that is often answered poorly.

Questions

1   Explain how two items of reprographics equipment/software (other than a photocopier) could be used by an organisation. (2 KU – G)

2   Brian Farmer, a reprographics assistant, has had difficulty in deciding how the following items which have already been photocopied should be finished.
    ◆   A multi-page staff newsletter.
    ◆   Health and safety posters to be displayed around the workplace.
    ◆   New pages which are to be added to the health and safety manual ring binder.

    Advise Brian on what equipment could be used to finish these documents. Give a different suggestion for each. You must state clearly one advantage of each piece of equipment. (6 PS – G)

3   The following problems have occurred in the Reprographics section of Gaga Ltd.
    ◆   Staff have complained that photocopying is not being completed according to their instructions.
    ◆   A Reprographics assistant received an electric shock when he tried to repair a broken photocopier.

    Suggest and justify how the above problems could be overcome. (4 PS – C)

4   Suggest two reasons why an organisation may choose to 'outsource'/use an external agency for some or all of their reprographics work? (2 KU – C)

5   Bargos plc wants to make 200 copies of a letter to be sent to customers. They are unsure whether to copy the letter in-house or whether to use an outside agency. Recommend which method would be best and give reasons for your answer. (4 PS – C)

SOURCES OF INFORMATION

Organisations use information every day for a variety of purposes. For example, they will require information on hotels, trains and taxis in order to make travel arrangements. They will need the telephone numbers for plumbers, electricians and repair engineers in order to carry out work around the office.

In order to find all the information needed by an organisation, an administration assistant will use three main sources. These are:

People-Based Sources: This involves talking to people in order to gain information. This may happen through meetings, telephone conversations or face-to-face discussions.

Paper-Based Sources: This involves accessing information that is held in paper form. For example, books, newspapers, dictionaries, manuals, instruction guides, encyclopaedias, atlases, phone books and Who's Who are all forms of paper-based information sources.

Hints and Tips

Many pupils knowledge of paper-based sources of information is poor. Make sure you are not one of them.

ICT-Based Sources: This involves accessing information that is held in digital form. For example, teletext, CD-ROMs, computer files, electronic diary, email, intranet and the internet are all forms of ICT-based information sources.

Choosing an Information Source

There are thousands and thousands of information sources available to an administration assistant. It is therefore vital that an administration assistant has some knowledge on which source of information is the most valuable in any given circumstance. If not, time and money will be wasted searching for information in the wrong place.

In the following circumstances the information sources below would be appropriate.

Customer Telephone Number: organisational database, telephone book, phone directory enquiries.

List of Tradesman (Plumbers, Electricians etc): the Yellow Pages, yell.com or organisational database.

Postcode Search: royalmail.com

List of Rich and Important People: Who's Who or Sunday Times Rich List

Train Times: Train timetable or nationalrail.co.uk

News Headlines: Teletext or bbc.co.uk

Exchange Rates: Bank, Post Office or xe.com

Location of a City: Atlas

Directions: Map or theaa.com route planner

Historical Information: Encyclopaedia or Old Copies of Newspapers on CD-ROMs

Intranet

An intranet is the name given to a computer network that operates within an organisation and which only employees of that organisation have access to. All information available on the intranet is stored by the organisation's server. Any computer that is part of the network has access to the files and software applications stored on the server.

As part of an intranet, an organisation may have a number of pages which include information on: staff telephone numbers, departmental details, vacancies, instruction guides and information on training courses. This area is often designed in the same format as an internet site.

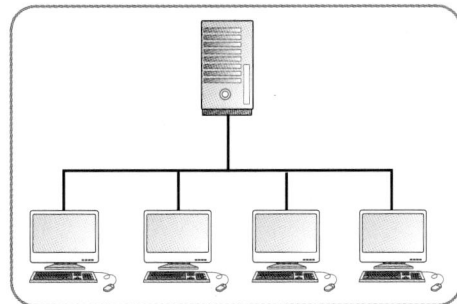

Figure 5.1 Intranet

By creating an intranet an organisation may benefit in the following ways: i) software applications such as Word, Excel, Access and PowerPoint can be shared by all employees as they are accessed through the organisation's server, ii) by sharing information over an intranet an organisation no longer needs to issue paper memos to every employee which will cut costs, iii) employees will find it easier to find information on an intranet as most have a search facility similar to those on the internet, iv) discussion forums, just like those on the internet, can be set up for employees to exchange ideas and discuss work-related issues (this should improve work flow), v) employees can access information on the intranet from any networked computer, and vi) new information can be added very quickly so employees are always aware of what is happening in the organisation.

Although an intranet is an effective way of sharing information there can be a number of problems. These include: i) setting up and designing an intranet can be costly, ii) staff will need to be trained in how to add new information to the intranet, and iii) if the network goes down, employees will not be able to access any information.

(!) Many pupils confuse an intranet with the internet. Be careful.

Internet

The internet is a communications and information network that links computers all over the world. The information that is available on the internet is stored on powerful servers that are owned by governments, universities, large commercial organisations or Internet Service Providers (ISPs) such as AOL and Virgin.

Unlike an intranet, the internet can be accessed from any computer anywhere in the world that has internet access. In order to access the internet the following equipment and software is needed: i) a computer, ii) a modem to connect to the phone line, iii) a phone line, iv) an account with an ISP, and v) internet software such as Microsoft Explorer or Netscape.

Internet Sites

Once access has been gained to the internet there are an abundance of sites which can be accessed. Although most sites provide information in the form of pages that can be moved between, a number of sites offer different facilities. These include chat rooms, email accounts, games and e-commerce. Nevertheless, the vast majority of sites provide information on such issues as the weather, sport, transport, current affairs, hobbies, companies and travel.

As there are so many internet sites it is important that each site has its own distinct web address. Without each page on a site having its own address, called a Uniform Resource Locator (URL), it would be impossible to access information quickly and efficiently.

Designing and Creating a Good Website

Just like a reception area, the design of an organisation's website is important in providing it with a positive image. However, designing a good website that is user friendly is very difficult. This is why many organisations will outsource the design and maintenance of their site to an internet design company. By doing this it is more likely that the site will contain the features of a good website that is user friendly.

The features of a good website include:

The Website Address

The address should be easy to remember. If possible the address should include the organisation's name or be connected to it in some way.

Colourful

A website should make use of colour in order to make it stand out. However, it should not be so colourful that it actually takes away from the information on the site.

Information

A site should contain information that is useful, honest and correct. The writing on a site should use a font style and font size that is readable. Pictures, graphics and charts can be used to help understanding and make the information more interesting.

Special Effects

To make a site stand out special effects may be added using Flash. However, care should be taken not to add special effects that cause a site to take a long time to load up.

Hyperlinks

There should be hyperlinks which provide direct access to other pages on the site or to another website. This makes a site more user friendly as information that is linked can be directly connected even though it is on two separate pages. It also saves the user having to type in new website addresses in order to move to another web page. Hyperlinks are usually identified with coloured writing or images which turn the cursor into a hand when passed over them.

Two types of hyperlink that may be displayed on a home page or in the footer of each page on a website are: i) Frequently Asked Questions (FAQs) hyperlink: this hyperlink takes the user to a web page that contains a list of questions that customers ask on a regular basis, and ii) Contact Us hyperlink: this hyperlink can be used by users to contact the organisation via email.

Search Engine Facility

Finding information on a website can be very difficult. By putting a search engine facility on their home page, an organisation makes it easier for users to find the information they want from the site quickly and efficiently. As with an internet wide search engine, all the user has to do is type in a keyword which the site engine then uses to locate the information the user is after.

E-commerce facility

In order to take advantage of those customers who wish to purchase online an organisation must offer an e-commerce facility on its site.

An example of a good web site (www.johnlewis.com) is shown below.

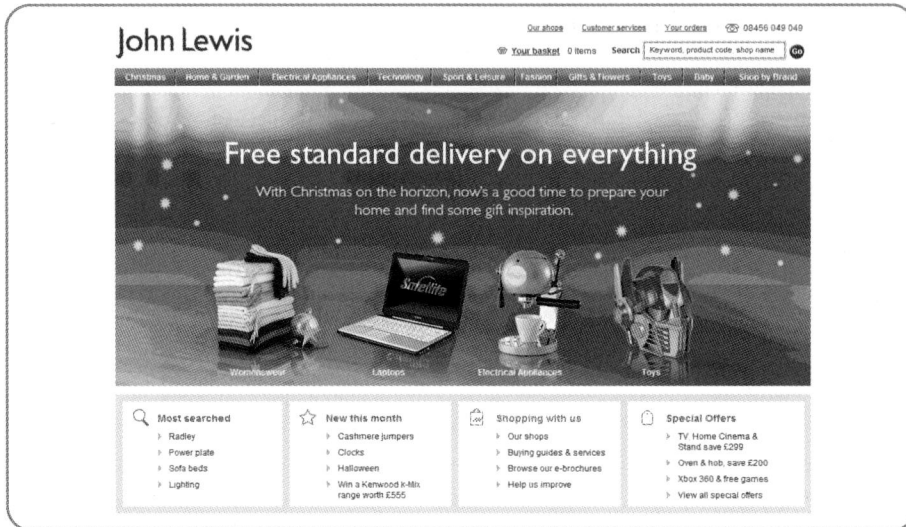

Figure 5.2 John Lewis Website

Selling Products Using the Internet

The internet is increasingly becoming a location where customers wish to purchase products and services from organisations. This process of purchasing and selling products online is called e-commerce.

Hints and Tips

Make sure you know the definition for e-commerce. It is a definition that pupils often describe poorly in the written exam.

E-commerce is popular with customers and organisations as it offers benefits to both. From a customer's perspective, these include: i) products can be purchased from home; ii) products are often cheaper than you would find on the High Street; and iii) more products to choose from. Some products that are not available in your local area can be purchased online.

From an organisation's perspective, these include: i) access to more customers: an organisation located in Scotland can sell products all over the world, ii) lower costs: an online retailer does not need to spend money on lots of shops or employees to sell their products, and iii) products can be sold 24 hours a day, 7 days a week. Unlike many shops which close at night, an internet site is open all the time.

However, although selling online can be beneficial to an organisation, it is not as easy or as straightforward as it sounds. In fact, to successfully sell online an organisation must: i) make customers aware of their website e.g. an organisation could advertise its website on the TV, on the side of its vans, on billboards or on all their headed notepaper, ii) display its products effectively: the website must contain pictures and full descriptions of all the products the organisation has for sale, iii) have a search engine facility so that customers can find the products they are looking for quickly, iv) have a shopping basket facility: this lets a customer put products they are interested in to one side while they browse through the rest of the site. When the customer is ready to purchase, all the items in the shopping basket are displayed on the checkout page of the website. At any time, items can be removed or deleted from the shopping basket, v) have a secure payment facility: when paying for products online customers need to feel confident that their credit card or debit card number will be kept confidential and secure, vi) make sure that products are delivered to the customer quickly and in good shape, and vii) have a fair returns policy which lets customers return faulty products cheaply and provides online refunds.

Using the Internet Effectively

With so many sites and so much information it would be virtually impossible to find anything on the internet by just randomly searching through it. This is why search engines such as Google, Yahoo, Ask and MSN were created.

A search engine is a facility which helps a user locate information on the internet. It works by matching the keywords the user has typed into the search engine against those in the search engine's database of internet sites. If a keyword match is found, the search engine creates a list of sites from which the user can choose. The list created is displayed as a web page with hyperlinks that provide direct access to the sites identified by the search engine. In most instances, the search engine will rank the sites according to how closely they match the keywords the user typed in.

Having found a useful internet site, it is important that a note is taken of its address so that it can be accessed at a future date if required. Although this could be done by writing the site name down, most Web Browser software packages have a facility which allows website addresses to be stored. For example, Microsoft's Internet Explorer has a toolbar facility called 'Favourites' where website addresses can be stored in folders under subject headings.

Some of the other popular features that are found on most Web Browser software packages include: i) a Back icon that allows the user to move backwards through the web pages they have just been on, ii) a Forward icon that allows the user to move forwards again having looked back at previous web pages, iii) a History icon that allows the user to access web pages that were entered on previous occasions they had been surfing (Web pages that were accessed anything up to 3 weeks ago are recorded), iv) a Home Page icon that returns the user to their home page from anywhere on the Internet, and v) a New Tab icon that allows the user to have several web pages open at the same time on different tabs.

How Can the Internet Assist Departments in an Organisation?

With search engines and web browser software becoming ever more powerful and sophisticated it is no wonder that organisations are increasingly using the internet to support their work. Specific departmental uses include:

Purchasing Department

The Purchasing department will use the internet to: i) search for new suppliers to find out what prices they charge, ii) to order stock online anytime of the day, and iii) to compare suppliers from all over the world.

Sales and Marketing Department

The Sales and Marketing Department will use the internet to: i) undertake market research of customers and other businesses, ii) to advertise products on the organisation's website, and iii) sell products on the organisation's website.

Human Resources Department

The Human Resources Department will use the internet to: i) advertise jobs online, ii) place training materials online for employees to use, and iii) research current human resources legislation.

Finance Department

The Finance Department will use the internet to: i) check and manage the organisation's bank accounts online, ii) complete tax returns online, iii) research current accounting practices, and iv) research different accounting firms.

Although the internet has assisted departmental performance, a number of organisations have become increasingly concerned that some employees are using it for personal use. In order to resolve this issue, some organisations have installed software which blocks certain websites from being loaded. Others, on the other hand, maintain a record of all sites that employees have accessed in order to ascertain whether they are using the Internet for personal or business use.

Questions ?

1 Describe two benefits to an organisation of introducing an intranet. (2 KU – C)

2 Explain the benefits to an organisation of having an e-commerce facility on their internet site. (3 KU – C)

3 Explain the following terms.
 ◆ Hyperlink
 ◆ Search Engine (2 KU – G)

4 Name and describe three features that should be included on a website to make it user-friendly. (3 KU – G)

5 The following complaints have been received by customers using Fluff Ltd's website:
 ◆ Products shown on the website cannot be purchased through the site.
 ◆ There is no way to contact the organisation via the website.
 ◆ Customers have given up looking for what they want on the website.

 Suggest a different solution to each of the problems identified above. (3 PS – G)

6 Describe how the Sales and Marketing Department could use the internet. (2 KU – G)

PREPARATION AND PRESENTATION OF INFORMATION

There are two phrases that are commonly associated with information. The first, 'Information is Power', implies that access to information can have a positive effect upon an organisation. The second, 'Information Overload', suggests that too much information can have a negative effect upon an organisation.

It therefore seems that organisations must be very careful in the way that they deal with information. Having access to lots of it is not enough. The real key is ensuring that information is prepared and presented in a way that makes it useful to whoever intends to use it.

Using ICT to Prepare and Present Information

Over the past 20 years, ICT has played an increasingly important role in document preparation and presentation. This does not mean that using paper and a pen has become redundant, just that using ICT allows documents to be prepared and presented in a more professional way.

The benefits of using ICT to prepare and present information include:

Changes and Alterations: Information can be altered quickly and easily without making a mess of the document.

Storage: Documents created using ICT can be easily saved and stored on a computer's hard drive, a CD or a flash drive.

Templates and Standard House Style: Templates can be placed on the network for use by employees. The templates created are usually designed using what is known as a standard house style. The benefits of using a standard house style include: i) all documents created by the organisation are the same and hence look very professional, ii) staff can be easily trained to use a standard house style, iii) staff will become very familiar with the standard house style meaning fewer mistakes and errors will be made, and iv) checking work will be easier as all documents are produced using an identical layout.

Hints *and* Tips

Make sure you know what a standard house style is. Pupils often struggle with this term in the written exam.

Software Applications: Software applications such Microsoft Excel, PowerPoint, Access and Word have a number of features which enhance the presentation of information. For example, Microsoft Excel allows charts to be made, whereas, Microsoft PowerPoint allows special effects to be added to presentations.

Hints *and* Tips

Make sure you know what a software application is. Pupils often struggle with this term in the written exam.

Equipment used in Preparing and Presenting Information

There are a number of pieces of equipment that can be used to help prepare and present information. Some of the most common are noted below:

Flipchart Pad

A flipchart pad is used during presentations or training sessions for writing key points on. Usually attached to a large clipboard, the flipchart pad is made up of either A2- or A1-sized paper. An assortment of coloured marker pens is used to write on such paper.

Overhead Projector (OHP)

An OHP is a device that magnifies an A4-sized document so that it can be displayed in an enlarged form on a screen. This is done by photocopying an A4 paper-based document onto an A4 acetate sheet. The acetate sheet is then placed on the top of an OHP before light is shone through it. The light image is then magnified before being reflected onto a white screen using a mirror. An OHP can be used for giving presentations that are to be viewed by many people.

Laminator

A laminator is a piece of equipment which coats paper or card in a thin film of clear plastic. Notices or displays are often laminated so that the information contained on them is protected from dirt or water.

Binder

A binder is a piece of equipment which allows a multi-page document to be fastened together using a plastic binder. By binding a document together it is less likely that pages will come loose and be lost. Reports, manuals and instruction booklets are usually bound.

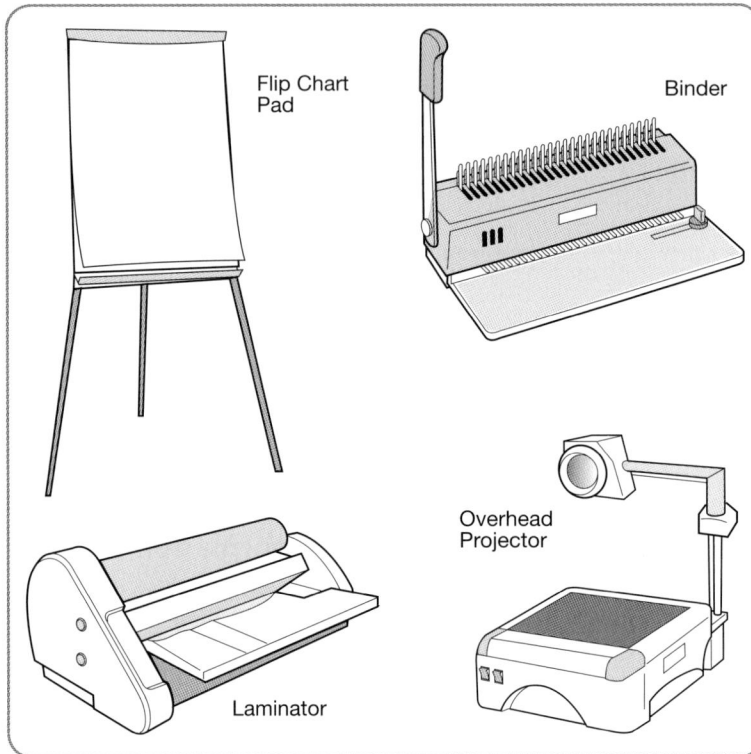

Figure 6.1 Equipment for preparing and presenting information

Scanner

A scanner is an electronic device which uses a light-sensitive scanning device to convert paper-based documents into a digital form. Once converted, the document or image can be saved as a computer file or copied into another document such as a report or a notice.

Printer

A printer is used to convert what has been created digitally on a computer or laptop into a paper-based form. There are two main types of printer: Inkjet and Laser. Although inkjet printers are cheap they have become less and less popular because they are slow and the print quality can be disappointing. Laser printers on the other hand are very fast and produce high-quality prints. Unfortunately, laser printers are rather expensive, especially if a colour one is purchased.

Projector

A projector is a device which when connected to a computer projects and enlarges what is displayed on the computer's monitor onto a whiteboard or screen. A projector is used for giving presentations, especially when there is a large audience that needs to see the information being displayed.

Interactive Whiteboard

An interactive whiteboard is a device that displays in enlarged form what is shown on a computer screen. However, unlike a traditional whiteboard, an interactive one has software programmed into it which acts in the same way as the computer's own mouse and keyboard. This allows a user to interact with the whiteboard instead of having to use the computer's mouse and keyboard. Interactive whiteboards are used during presentations or training sessions.

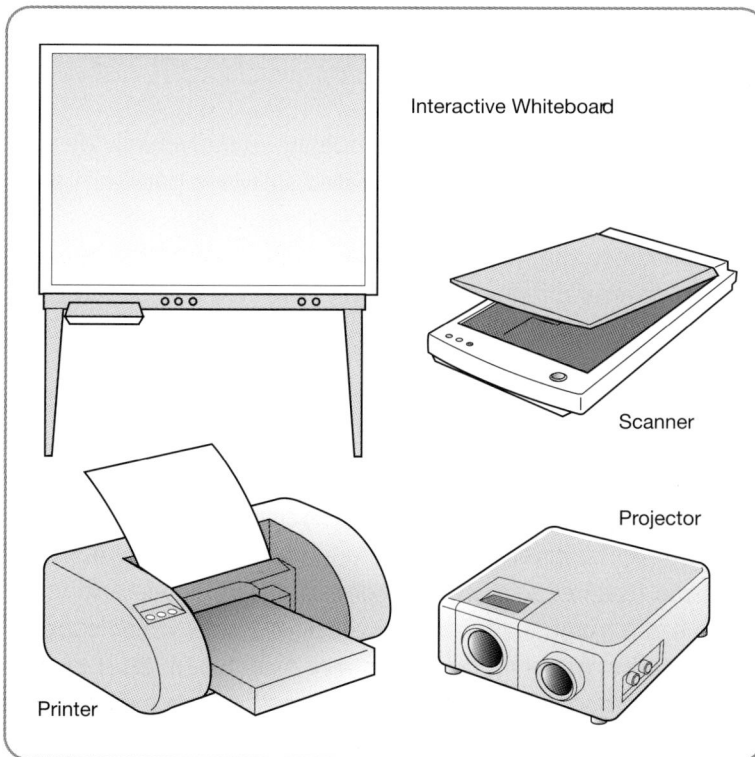

Interactive Whiteboard

Scanner

Projector

Printer

Figure 6.2 More equipment for preparing and presenting information

Software Used in Preparing and Presenting Information

Most software that is used in the preparation and presentation of information will be part of an integrated software package such as Microsoft Office. Such packages are made up of different software applications which are designed to carry out certain tasks. For example, Microsoft's PowerPoint software application is designed to help create presentations, whereas Microsoft's Access software application aids in the preparation of databases.

Hints and Tips

Make sure you know what an integrated software package is. Pupils often struggle with this term in the written exam.

The benefits of using an integrated software package are: i) the purchase of the package is often cheaper than buying software applications individually, ii) information can be easily transferred and linked between applications within the package. For example, Microsoft allows information from an Access database to be merged with a word processed letter in Word, iii) each application in the package is designed in a similar way. This makes it easier for employees to learn how to use each application. For example, in each application of Microsoft, the instruction to 'Print' is found in the File menu, and iv) different applications in the package can be open at the same time.

The drawbacks of using an integrated software package are: i) individually designed software can sometimes be more expensive, ii) integrated software packages are constantly being updated. To maintain the most up-to-date software, an organisation will have to purchase the new package, and iii) integrated software packages can suffer from technical difficulties that affect the way in which they function.

Microsoft's integrated software package has several applications which can be used in the preparation and presentation of information. The most common are:

Microsoft Word

Microsoft Word is a word processing software application used to produce documents such as letters, reports, itineraries, forms and memorandums. Although full of basic word processing features such as underline, bold, font style and font size, Microsoft Word also has a number of more advanced features which support the preparation and presentation of such documents. For example, a letter can be prepared in Word and then merged with data from a Microsoft Access database. Templates, such as an organisational letterhead, can be set up for use by employees. Tables can be created which help to display statistical information in a more effective manner.

The benefits of using Microsoft Word to present and prepare information:
i) information can be easily updated and altered without making a mess of the document, ii) a number of features are available in Word which improve the presentation of any document created e.g. underline, bold, tables etc., and
iii) templates can be designed which employees can use to produce high-quality and professional-looking documents.

Microsoft Excel

Microsoft Excel is a spreadsheet software application used to display numbers and carry out calculations. Made up of sheets layered one on top of the other, each sheet contains a number of cells which are set out in columns denoted by letters, and rows denoted by numbers. As every column and row is named it means that every cell on a spreadsheet has a cell reference. For example, cell B2 is highlighted in the sheet below. Furthermore, it is possible to format each one differently. For example, the number in cell A3 has been formatted as currency, whereas the number in cell C3 has been formatted as a percentage.

As well as being able to format information, Microsoft Excel has a number of other more advanced features. For example, formulas can be used to make calculations. As the example below shows, every formula begins with an equals sign (=) and cell references are used instead of typing in the numbers.

	A	B	C
1			
2		cell B2	
3	£15		25%

Figure 6.3 Excel spreadsheet

	A	B	C	D
1				
2	254	multiplied by	45	A2*C2
3				

Figure 6.4 Excel spreadsheet

Charts or diagrams can also be made using Microsoft Excel. This is a particularly useful function as displaying statistical information in a chart makes it easier to: i) understand the information, ii) compare the information to find out which month or period had the best figures and which had the worse, and iii) identify trends in the figures. Are they rising or are they falling?

There are many different chart or diagram types that can be created. Some of the most common are a line graph, a pictogram, a bar chart and a pie chart. A line graph and a pictogram are shown below.

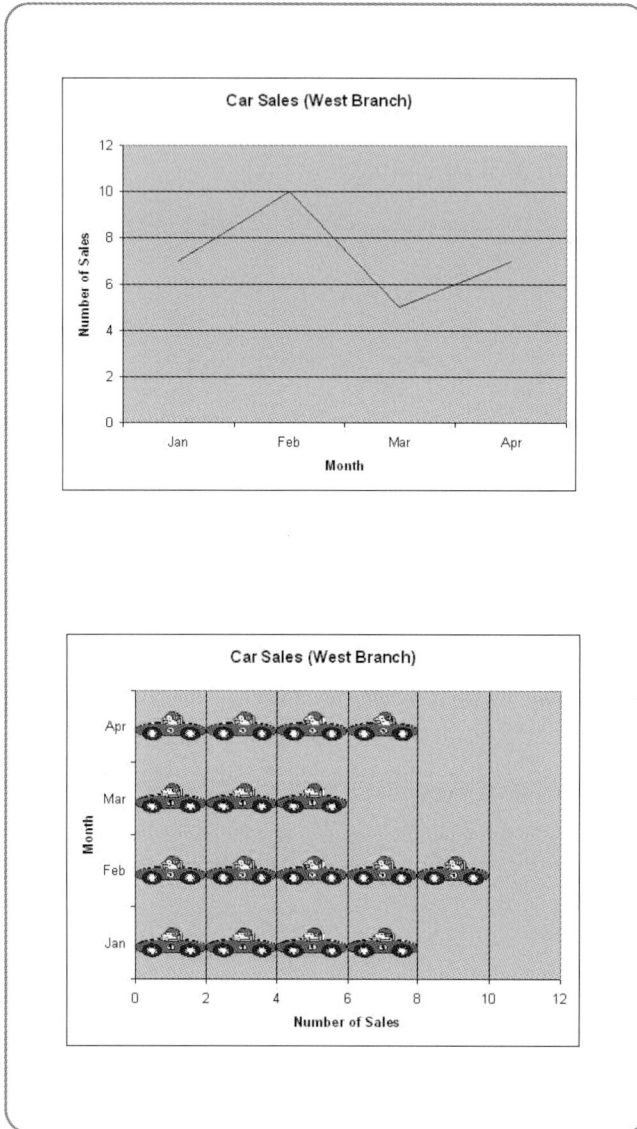

Figure 6.5 Excel charts

The benefits of using Microsoft Excel to present and prepare information are:
i) information can be updated and amended easily and without making a mess of the spreadsheet. For example, new rows and columns can be added to a spreadsheet, ii) calculated figures automatically update if formulas are used, iii) formulas can be copied into cells automatically using the auto fill function, iv) statistical information can be displayed as a chart, v) a number of features are available in Excel which improve the presentation of any spreadsheet created e.g.

underline, bold, borders, shading etc., and vi) each cell can be formatted to display information in a certain way e.g. as currency, as a percentage or as a date.

Microsoft Access

Microsoft Access is a database software application used to store information. For example, an organisation may create a database that contains the details of all its customers or the details of all its suppliers. The information in the database is set up in a table format, where each column is called a field and each row a record. Within each field, similar information is inputted, such as all employees' first names. Within each record, information for a particular employee, customer or supplier is inputted.

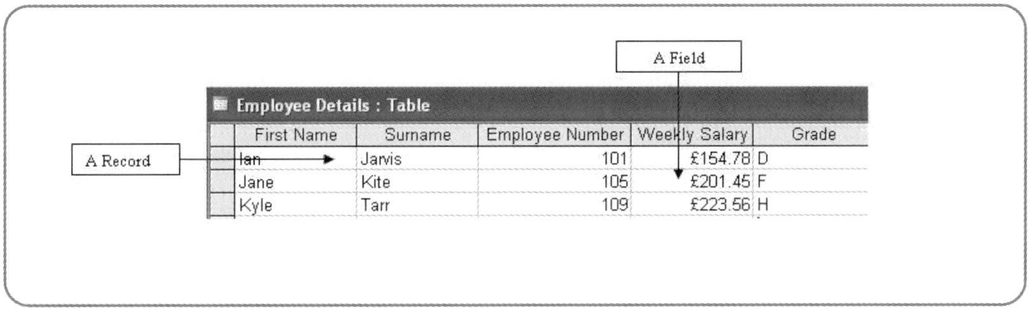

Figure 6.6 Access database

When setting up a database it is important that each field does not contain too much information. For example: i) address information should be split into Street, Town and Post Code fields, and ii) a person's name should be split into First Name and Surname fields.

As with a spreadsheet, information in an Access database can be formatted. For example, fields can be formatted as text, a number, a date or as currency. In the database above the Employee Number field has been formatted as a number and the Weekly Salary has been formatted as currency.

Microsoft Access also has a number of other features which allow the information to be sorted, searched through, filtered and queried.

The benefits of using Microsoft Access to present and prepare information are: i) information in a database can be easily deleted, updated and amended without making a mess, ii) fields in a database can be formatted to display information in a certain way e.g. as currency or as a date, iii) selected information can be searched for and then presented professionally and neatly in a Query or a Report, iv) information can be sorted into alphabetical or numerical order very easily, v) it is easier to keep information in an Access database neat and tidy than it would be if the information was stored manually in filing cabinets, vi) information stored in an Access database can be located far more quickly and easily than if stored in filing cabinets. This makes it a lot easier to prepare and present information, and

vii) information stored in an Access database can be merged with other software packages such as Word. For example, names and addresses in a database could be merged with a word processed letter in order to create personalised letters to be sent to all an organisation's customers.

Microsoft Publisher

Microsoft Publisher is a desktop publishing software application which can be used to create notices, adverts, magazines, business cards and such like. Made up of pre-designed templates, Microsoft Publisher allows text, graphics and photographs to be added to the templates in order to enhance their presentation. As well as many basic features such as underline and bold, Publisher also gives the user greater control over the placement of objects on the page.

The benefits of using Microsoft Publisher to present and prepare information are: i) a number of features are available in Publisher which improve the presentation of any document created e.g. WordArt, text boxes, bold, tables etc., ii) information can be altered, edited and deleted without making a mess of the document, and iii) templates are available which employees can use to produce high-quality and professional-looking documents e.g. letterheads, business cards, adverts, posters.

Microsoft PowerPoint

Microsoft PowerPoint is a presentation software application which can be used to create professional-looking presentations. Made up of pre-designed slide templates from which the user can choose, Microsoft PowerPoint allows text, graphics, charts and photographs to be added to each slide in order to enhance their presentation. As well as many basic features such as change of font size and font colour, PowerPoint also allows the user to add special effects, slide transitions and slide backgrounds to a presentation.

The benefits of using Microsoft PowerPoint to present and prepare information are: i) a number of features are available in PowerPoint which improve the presentation of any document created e.g. slide background, slide transition, custom animation, bold, font colour etc., ii) information can be altered, edited and deleted without making a mess of the presentation, iii) slide templates are available which employees can use to produce high-quality and professional-looking presentations, and iv) statistical information can be displayed in a presentation very easily.

Microsoft Outlook

Microsoft Outlook is a communications and personal organiser software application which can be used to send and receive emails, store email addresses, make

appointments and record tasks to be done. As well as the basic features outlined, Microsoft Outlook allows a user to manage their email account. For example, automatic emails can be set up to respond to messages which are received when an employee is out of the office.

The benefits of using Microsoft Outlook to prepare and present information are: i) an email message can be prepared and sent very quickly at virtually no cost, ii) messages can be prepared and sent with a flag that indicates how important the message is, iii) messages can be prepared with a tracking option which lets the user know when their message has been received and read, iv) a user can set up their inbox to display their email messages in a number of different ways. For example, in date received order or in alphabetical order, v) information held in the calendar, task, contacts and notes functions can be easily updated and altered without making a mess, and vi) messages can be sent with attachments.

The drawback of using Microsoft Outlook to prepare and present information is that email messages are often seen as an informal way of presenting and communicating a message.

Questions

1 Explain two benefits to an organisation of using a standard house style in the preparation of documents. (2 KU – G)

2 Jack Babacus is to give a sales presentation to his sales team. Justify the use of two pieces of equipment that Jack would need to give the presentation. (2 KU – C)

3 A number of health and safety posters are to be displayed in the staff room of Yahaa Ltd. Suggest two items of equipment which could be used to produce these posters. (2 KU – G)

4 Explain two benefits to an organisation of using an integrated software package. (2 KU – G)

5 Peter Jones is a Sales Manager at Scotty Lets Ltd. He often gives presentations to his team on sales performance. Unfortunately some members of his team have complained that displaying sales figures in a table on a flipchart is difficult to read and understand. Recommend two items of software that Peter could use to improve his presentations and justify your recommendations. (4 PS – C)

6 Describe two advantages of using an electronic database to store suppliers' details. (2 KU – G)

Questions continued ➤

Questions *continued* ?

7 After a recent review the following problems have been identified at LoLo Ltd.

◆ Time was wasted keying in 250 personalised letters to customers concerning an upcoming sale.

◆ Monthly profit figures are calculated manually. A number of mistakes have been made recently.

◆ A number of handwritten advertisements are displayed around the office. They look tacky and unprofessional.

Suggest and justify how the above problems may be overcome. (3 PS – C)

8 Cells in a spreadsheet are often formatted. Suggest two ways in which cells could be formatted. (2 KU – G)

9 Describe three benefits of using email. (3 KU – G)

10 Justify the use of a line graph to display sales figures. (1 KU – G)

11 Suggest two ways in which statistical information could be displayed effectively. (2 KU – G)

12 The following is an extract from the employee database of Jarside plc. The names have been sorted alphabetically.

Name	Department	Job Title	DoB	Date Started	Grading
Andrew Zacs	Finance	Manager	5/6/60	5/12/88	F
Brenda Johns	Personnel	Wages Clerk	22/6/70	6/7/98	C
Chris Popel	Administration	Manager	13/10/67	7/7/92	F

Recommend and justify an improvement to the structure of this database (2 PS – C)

13 Give an appropriate field type when formatting the field 'DoB' in the database above. (1 KU – G)

TRAVEL: ARRANGEMENTS

Arranging a business trip is one of the most demanding tasks that an administration assistant will undertake. This is because there are so many different issues that need to be considered in order to complete the task successfully.

What Factors Should be Considered when Making Arrangements for a Business Trip?

There are a number of factors that should be taken into account when making travel arrangements. The most important are noted below.

Name of Person Travelling
This information is important so that hotels and travel tickets can be booked correctly in the traveller's name. Without such information the booking may be made incorrectly meaning the traveller will have difficulty checking in at a hotel or for a flight.

The Destination
This information is important for several reasons: i) so the administration assistant can make travel and accommodation arrangements for the correct destination, ii) so that the most appropriate method of travel can be decided. For example, if flying from Edinburgh to Rome, a flight would be needed. However, if travelling from Edinburgh to Glasgow, a train could be taken, iii) so the administration assistant can find out if the traveller will need: foreign currency and what type, a passport and visa and immunisation from certain diseases e.g. yellow fever, typhoid.

Travel Dates and Times
This information is important for several reasons: i) so that hotels, flights and train tickets are booked correctly. Without it, hotels may be booked for the wrong days and flights may be booked that get the traveller to their destination far too early or even worse, far too late, ii) so the administration assistant can prepare an itinerary.

Time Available for Travelling
This information is important as it will influence what method of travel is chosen. If the employee only has a few hours available a flight may be chosen, whereas, if they have all day the employee may be willing to drive to their destination.

Details of Trip
This information is important so that the administration assistant can make the most suitable travel arrangements. For example, if the traveller is attending a

conference, a hotel nearby should be booked. On the other hand, if the traveller intends to visit a number of customers while away a hire car will need to be booked.

Company Policy

This information is important because many organisations have strict rules on what travel and accommodation arrangements can be made. For example, some companies only allow employees to travel economy while flying; others may only allow employees to stay in bed and breakfast accommodation while travelling.

Budget Available

This information is important as sometimes an administration assistant will only have a certain amount of money available to make travel and accommodation arrangements. If this is the case the administration assistant may have to book budget airline tickets or look for special offers on accommodation.

Position of Employee

This information is important because in some organisations, senior managers are given certain privileges. For example, a senior manager may be entitled to fly business class, whereas a normal employee would only be allowed an economy ticket.

Personal Preference

This information is important because some employees like to stay at the same hotel or catch a particular flight when they are on a business trip to a particular city.

Special Requirements

This information is important because the employee who is travelling may be disabled or have special dietary requirements. If this is the case, the administration assistant will have to make any hotel or airline booked aware of this so that the appropriate arrangements can be made.

Travel and Accommodation Availability

This information is important because at certain times of the year e.g. bank holidays, Christmas, travel and accommodation bookings are far harder to make because demand is high. This is also the case if a big conference or exhibition is taking place in a particular city. The administration assistant will therefore have to make any bookings for those times of the year well in advance so that they do not miss out.

Cancellation Policy

This information is important as business trips often need to be cancelled or amended close to the departure time. The administration assistant should therefore avoid making arrangements with hotels, airlines or train companies where cancellations or amendments can not be made, or where it costs to do so.

How is Information Collected from an Employee for a Business Trip?

To successfully organise a business trip an administration assistant needs to collect a considerable amount of information from the employee who is travelling. In order that this is done accurately a travel/accommodation request form is usually completed. On the form, the employee is asked a number of questions which will help the administration assistant make the necessary travel arrangements. A travel/accommodation request form is shown below:

TRAVEL/ACCOMMODATION REQUEST FORM	
EMPLOYEE DETAILS	
Name	John Drummond
Job title	Sales and Marketing Director
TRAVEL DETAILS	
Preferred Method of Travel	Train
Special Requests	First class ticket
Outward Journey	
Departure Date	22 August 2008
Place of Departure	Edinburgh
Place of Arrival	Manchester
Preferred Time of Arrival	1900 hours
Return Journey	
Return Date	23 August 2008
Place of Departure	Manchester
Place of Arrival	Edinburgh
Preferred Time of Departure	1700 hours
ACCOMODATION DETAILS	
Accommodation Required	Hotel
Date of Arrival	22 August 2008
Date of Departure	23 August 2008
Special Requests	None
Signed	John Drummond
Date	10 August 2008

Organising a Business Trip

Once a travel/accommodation request form has been completed an administration assistant can then start to organise the business trip. There are two main steps in this process:

Collection and Analysis of Travel and Accommodation Information

Before any arrangements can be made it is important to discover what travel and accommodation options are available. The main sources of information that an administration assistant will use are:

Paper-Based Sources: For example, bus and train timetables, AA and RAC handbooks, hotel chain guides.

The benefits of using such sources are: i) the information tends to be accurate, especially the information contained in timetables and AA/RAC handbooks. If using a timetable it is important to check that it is the most recent version so that travel arrangements may be made correctly, ii) timetables are designed in a way that makes them straightforward and easy to use, and iii) some people prefer reading information from paper than a computer screen.

People-Based Sources: For example travel agents and feedback from employees.

The benefits of using such sources are: i) travel agents may be able to obtain discounted deals, ii) travel agents are specialists in arranging travel and accommodation meaning the process should run smoothly, and iii) feedback from employees should provide a fair and honest opinion of any airlines, train companies, hire car companies and hotels previously used.

ICT-Based Sources: For example the internet or teletext.

The benefits of using such sources are: i) cheap, last minute deals can be obtained on the internet and teletext, ii) many internet sites provide pictures or video clips of their hotels, and iii) up-to-date information on timetables and accommodation is easily accessed on line.

Making the Travel and Accommodation Arrangements

Once all the travel and accommodation information has been collected, the administration assistant will then be responsible for make the necessary bookings. There are a number of different ways that this could be done:

Telephone: A telephone may be used to contact a travel agent, hotel, airline or car hire company in order to make a booking or purchase tickets.

Online: If the hotel, airline or car hire company have an e-commerce facility, then bookings may be made or tickets purchased directly over the internet.

Fax: A fax may be used to send a travel and accommodation booking form to a travel agent or directly to a hotel or airline. The form that would be sent would look similar to the one shown below:

When making the bookings a number of factors should be taken into account. These include: i) making sure enough time is set aside between travel bookings. By doing this the employee will not have to rush if there is a slight delay along their route or if they have to transfer between airport terminals, ii) how travel and accommodations bookings will be paid for. Should the organisation be invoiced directly or will the employee pay and then complete an expenses claim form?, and iii) what confirmation e.g. letter, email, fax, should be requested when making the bookings?

HOW TO PASS STANDARD GRADE ADMINISTRATION

TRAVEL/ACCOMMODATION ORDER FORM	
Abacus Enterprises 22 Kessop Street Edinburgh EH4 9TH	
To: GoGo Travel 23 Locket Street Edinburgh EH10 7TY	
Please book the following travel and accommodation arrangements. Please send the invoice to the above address.	
EMPLOYEE DETAILS	
Name:	John Drummond
Job Title:	Sales and Marketing Director
TRAVEL DETAILS	
Destination:	Manchester
Departure date:	22 August 2008
Departure time:	1710 hours
Return date:	23 August 2008
Return time:	1725 hours
Preferred form of travel:	Train
Special requests:	First class ticket
ACCOMMODATION DETAILS	
Name and address of accommodation:	The Dodsworth Hotel 23 Jarvy Road Manchester M4 7TG
Number of nights accommodation:	One
Special request(s):	None
Signed:	Harry Joppa (Travel Administration Assistant)
Date:	12 August 2008

Making an Employee Aware of their Travel and Accommodation Arrangements

Once everything has been booked it is important that an itinerary is produced which outlines all the travel and accommodation details as well as any appointments that the employee may have while on their business trip.

As an employee will use the itinerary while travelling it is important that it is easy to understand and makes sense. To ensure this, the administration assistant should: i) indicate the dates of travel, ii) put all the travel, accommodation and appointment plans in date and time order, iii) use the 24-hour clock to show times, iv) include all departure and arrival times, v) include, where necessary, the name, address and telephone number of all hotels, travel companies and appointments on the itinerary, and vi) include all airline check-in times, flight numbers and terminal numbers where available.

An example of a completed itinerary is shown below:

ITINERARY	
Mr John Smart – Sales Manager	
Edinburgh to Luton	
24 September 2008	
Time	Details
0800 hours	Taxi from home to Edinburgh Airport (already booked)
0830 hours	Arrive at Edinburgh Airport
0845 hours	Check in for EasyJet flight to Luton (Flight Number EZ2361)
1000 hours	Flight departs
1100 hours	Flight arrives at Luton
1130 hours	Catch a taxi outside the Airport to Typhoon Enterprises, 23 North Street, Luton
1200 hours	Arrive at Typhoon Enterprises for meeting with Mr Barry Tellor, Managing Director
1400 hours	Depart Typhoon Enterprises for Luton Airport by taxi
1430 hours	Arrive at Luton Airport
1445 hours	Check in for EasyJet flight to Edinburgh (Flight Number EZ4382)
1600 hours	Flight departs
1700 hours	Flight arrives at Edinburgh
1730 hours	Catch taxi outside Airport and return home

Business Trips Abroad

Although most business trips take place within the UK, a significant number will involve international travel. If this is the case, the administration assistant should make the employee aware of a number of important documents that will be required when travelling abroad. These include:

A Passport: This is absolutely essential. Without a valid passport an employee will be unable to pass through customs points and will be sent home.

A Visa: When travelling to some countries a visa is required for entry. Without a valid visa an employee will be unable to pass through customs points and will be sent home. In many countries, the visa can be completed on arrival; however, in others a visa is required before even travelling.

European Health Insurance Card (EHIC): This card is important as it entitles the employee to free emergency medical treatment in all European Union countries.

Travel Insurance documentation: This documentation is important as it can be used to obtain health care and legal assistance whilst abroad. Travel insurance is of particular use while travelling in non-European Union countries.

Driving License: A full UK driving license will be needed if the employee intends to hire a car while abroad.

As well as the documentation noted above, an administration assistant should ensure the employee: i) is immunised against any diseases that exist in the country being visited e.g. yellow fever, polio, typhoid, ii) has a phrase book to help with communication, iii) has some foreign currency in order to pay for minor expenses, iv) has an emergency contact number and a mobile phone that allows international calls to be made, and v) has a map of the area being visited so they do not get lost.

Questions **?**

1 Justify the use of one paper-based source of information when making arrangements for a business trip. (1 KU – C)

2 Jerry Tate is a newly appointed Administration Assistant at Mars Exporters plc, based in Glasgow. He received the following memo today.

MEMORANDUM

To: Jerry Tate

From: John Barr, Sales and Marketing Director

Date: 12 June 2008

Subject: Trip to Rome for Product Exhibition

I will be attending the above product exhibition in Rome. I need to depart on Monday 23 June and return on Wednesday 25 June. I want to stay in a 4-star hotel near to where the product exhibition is taking place.

I would like you to make all the necessary arrangements.

As Jerry has very little experience he has asked you for help in completing this task. Suggest and justify three pieces of advice you would give Jerry to help organise the trip. Give a different justification for each piece of advice. (6 PS – C)

3 Other than a passport, suggest and justify two documents that could be used when making a business trip abroad. (4 KU – C)

TRAVEL: PAYING FOR BUSINESS TRIPS

When arranging payment for travel and accommodation an administration assistant can request one of two things:

- That the invoice be sent directly to the organisation for payment.
- That the invoice will be settled by the employee:
  - i) On departure from the hotel.
  - ii) On collection of their travel tickets.

Whichever method is chosen there are a number of different ways in which payment can be made.

Company Cheque

A company cheque is usually used when an organisation requests that they be invoiced directly. The benefits of using a cheque are: i) the employee does not have to be worried about making payment for travel or accommodation while on their business trip, ii) when writing the cheque, the administration assistant will note the name of the business and amount that has been sent on the cheque tab. This makes it easy to maintain a record of business expenses.

Personal Cheque

If an employee has to pay their own expenses they may use a personal cheque. However, many hotels, garages and travel companies will not accept a personal cheque unless it is accompanied with a cheque guarantee card. The benefits of using a personal cheque are: i) the employee will not have to carry large amounts of cash which is safer, ii) when writing the cheque, the employee will note the name of the business and amount that has been paid on the cheque tab. This will make it easier to complete an expenses claim form on the employee's return.

Cash

Cash is used to pay for small expenses such as taxi fares, underground tickets and snacks while travelling. The benefits of using cash are: i) paying with cash is easy and convenient, and ii) some taxis, buses and shops will only accept cash, especially if the cost is under £5.

Business Credit Card

A business credit card can be used by an administration assistant to pay for travel and accommodation over the phone or online. An employee may also carry a business credit card to pay for travel and accommodation while on their trip. The benefits of using a business credit card are: i) the employee will not have to carry large amounts of cash which is safer, ii) they are very secure. A pin number or a security code on the back of the card is required before a payment is authorised, iii) expenses are easy to track because a bill is sent to the organisation at the end of each month, iv) they can be used abroad.

Debit Card

A debit card can be used by an administration assistant to pay for travel and accommodation over the phone or online. An employee may also carry a debit card to pay for travel and accommodation while on their trip. The benefits of using a debit card are: i) the employee will not have to carry large amounts of cash which is safer, ii) they are very secure. A pin number or a security code on the back of the card is required before a payment is authorised, iii) expenses are easy to track because a statement of account will be sent to the organisation at the end of each month, iv) they can be used to withdraw cash from an autoteller.

Travellers' Cheques

Travellers' cheques are used when an employee is on a business trip abroad. The cheques are accepted as payment for most expenses and can also be converted into the local currency. The benefits of using travellers' cheques are: i) they are more secure than cash. A signature and identification are required before the travellers' cheques will be accepted, ii) if lost or stolen they can usually be replaced within 24 hours, iii) they can be converted into local currency by banks and many hotels.

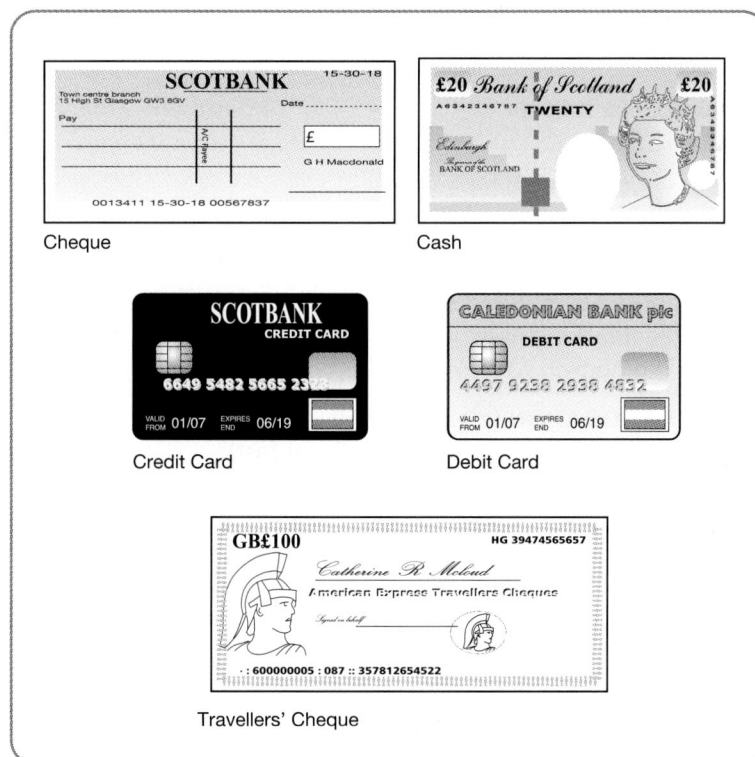

Figure 7.1 Methods of paying for travel

Expenses Claim Form

In most cases business trip expenses are paid using either a business credit card or by billing the organisation directly. However, in some instances an employee may have to pay certain expenses using their own money e.g. taxi fares, snacks. If this is the case, the employee should complete an expenses claim form on their return in order that they can be reimbursed.

When completing an expenses claim form it is important that the employee attaches receipts of all their expenses. Without receipts, an employee may have their claim turned down because they have no evidence that certain expenses were actually incurred.

The benefits of using an expenses claim form are: i) the organisation can use the forms to track and keep a record of business expenses, ii) using a standard form makes it easy for employees to claim back expenses, iii) using a standard from makes it easy and straightforward for finance staff to check claims, iv) the form outlines what can be claimed for and what is needed for a successful claim e.g. receipts.

An example of a completed expenses claim form is shown below:

EXPENSE CLAIM FORM		
All receipts and invoices should be attached where available		
Name: Jane Karstair	Department: Finance	
Date: 13/9/08 – 15/9/08	Total Expenditure	
	£	pp
TRAVEL (please detail) Train (Edinburgh to Newcastle return)	85	00
ACCOMMODATION (please detail) Barfield Hotel (2 nights Bed and Breakfast)	140	00
MEALS (please detail) Dinner x 2 (£18 + £20)	38	00
OTHER EXPENSES (please detail) Taxi x 4 (£7 + £5 + £6 + £6)	24	00
TOTAL EXPENSES DUE	287	00
Employee's Signature: Jane Karstair	Date: 18/9/08	

Questions **?**

1 A business credit card is often used to pay for business expenses while on a trip. Suggest two other methods of paying for business expenses. (2 KU – G)

2 Explain two benefits of using a business credit card. (2 KU – G)

3 Tommy Ball is a Sales Manager at HaVar Foods Ltd. He has recently been on a business trip to London where he paid the following expenses. Use the information below to complete an Expenses Claim Form.

Dorset Hotel
23 Low Road
London
W4 7YU

Account Number: 34581
Room Number: 34
Customer Name: Tommy Ball (HaVar Foods Ltd)

Date	Details	Cost
26/8/08	Bed and Breakfast	£75.00
	Dinner	£15.00
	Bar Bill	£5.00
27/08/08	Bed and Breakfast	£75.00
	Dinner	£15.00
	Bar Bill	£10.00
TOTAL BILL (VAT @ 17.5% included)		**£195.00**

Paid with Thanks
Dorset Hotel

AA Taxis Receipt
26/8/08
£5.00

AA Taxis Receipt
27/8/08
£5.50

EASYAIR
Glasgow to London Return
26/08/08 – 28/08/08
£125
Received with thanks

Questions continued ➤

Questions *continued*

?

EXPENSE CLAIM FORM			
All receipts and invoices should be attached where available			
Name:	Department:		
Date:		Total Expenditure	
TRAVEL (please detail)		£	pp
ACCOMMODATION (please detail)			
MEALS (please detail)			
OTHER EXPENSES (please detail)			
TOTAL EXPENSES DUE			
Employee's Signature: *Tommy Ball*		Date: *2/10/08*	

PRACTICAL ABILITIES

As part of the Standard Grade Administration exam all candidates are required to undertake a Practical Abilities project. As part of the project every candidate is required to complete a number of tasks which challenges their ability to prepare and present information.

The way in which candidates prepare and present information is assessed in two main ways. These are:

Keyboarding Skills: Keyboarding skills assess how accurately and consistently a candidate inputs information on a task.

Function Skills: Function skills assess how well a candidate uses the features of a software application. For example, in Microsoft Word, appropriate use of underline or bold would demonstrate a function skill.

Keyboarding Skills

Unlike the vast majority of marking that takes place in an exam, keyboarding skills are marked negatively. What this means is that marks can only be lost, not gained. For example, in the Practical Abilities project, five marks may be allocated for keyboarding skills on a particular task. This means that if the candidate makes no keyboarding errors they will score five marks. However, if two mistakes are made, two marks will be deducted meaning the candidate only scores three marks. Of course, should a candidate make five or more errors, no marks will be awarded for the task. It is therefore absolutely vital that a candidate takes care when inputting information during a task.

How are Keyboarding Skills Marks Lost?

Keyboarding skills marks are lost for a number of reasons. The main problem areas are:

◆ Spelling words incorrectly
◆ Inputting the wrong information
◆ Inputting inappropriate information
◆ Forgetting to input information
◆ Not being able to see information
◆ Using lower and/or upper case letters incorrectly

- Using lower and/or upper case letters inconsistently
- Using abbreviations or timings inconsistently
- Incorrect spacing
- Inconsistent spacing
- Inconsistent use of font styles or font sizes
- Inconsistent formatting.

Example

To understand how easily keyboarding errors are made it is best to look at some actual examples:

Word Processing Example: An Itinerary

ITINERARY
Mr John Smart – Sales Manager
Edinburgh to Luton
24 September 2008

Time	Details
0800 hours	Taxi from home to Edinburgh Airport (already booked)
0830 hours	Arrive at Edinburgh Airport
0845 hours	Check in for EasyJet flight to Luton (Flight Number EZ2361)
10.00 hours	Flight departs
11.00 hours	Flight arrives at Luton
11.30 hours	Catch a taxi outside the Airport to Typhoon Enterprises, 23 North Street, Luton
1200 hours	Arrive at Typhoon Enterprises for meeting with Mr Barry Tellor, Managing Director
1400 hours	Depart Typhoon Enterprises for Luton Airport by taxi.
1430 hours	Arrive at Luton Airport
1445 hours	Check in for EasyJet flight to Edinburgh (Flight Number EZ4382)
1500 hours	Flight departs
1600 hours	Flight arrives at Edinburgh
1630 hours	Catch taxi outside Airport and return home

Inconsistent use of timings: All the times should be displayed without a full stop between the hours and the minutes.

Inconsistent spacing: There should be one empty line after each entry.

Wrong information: There should be no full stop at the end of an entry.

Inappropriate Time: Check-in must be at least half an hour before flight departure.

Figure 8.1 A travel itinerary

Example continued ➤

Example continued

Word Processing Example: A Letter

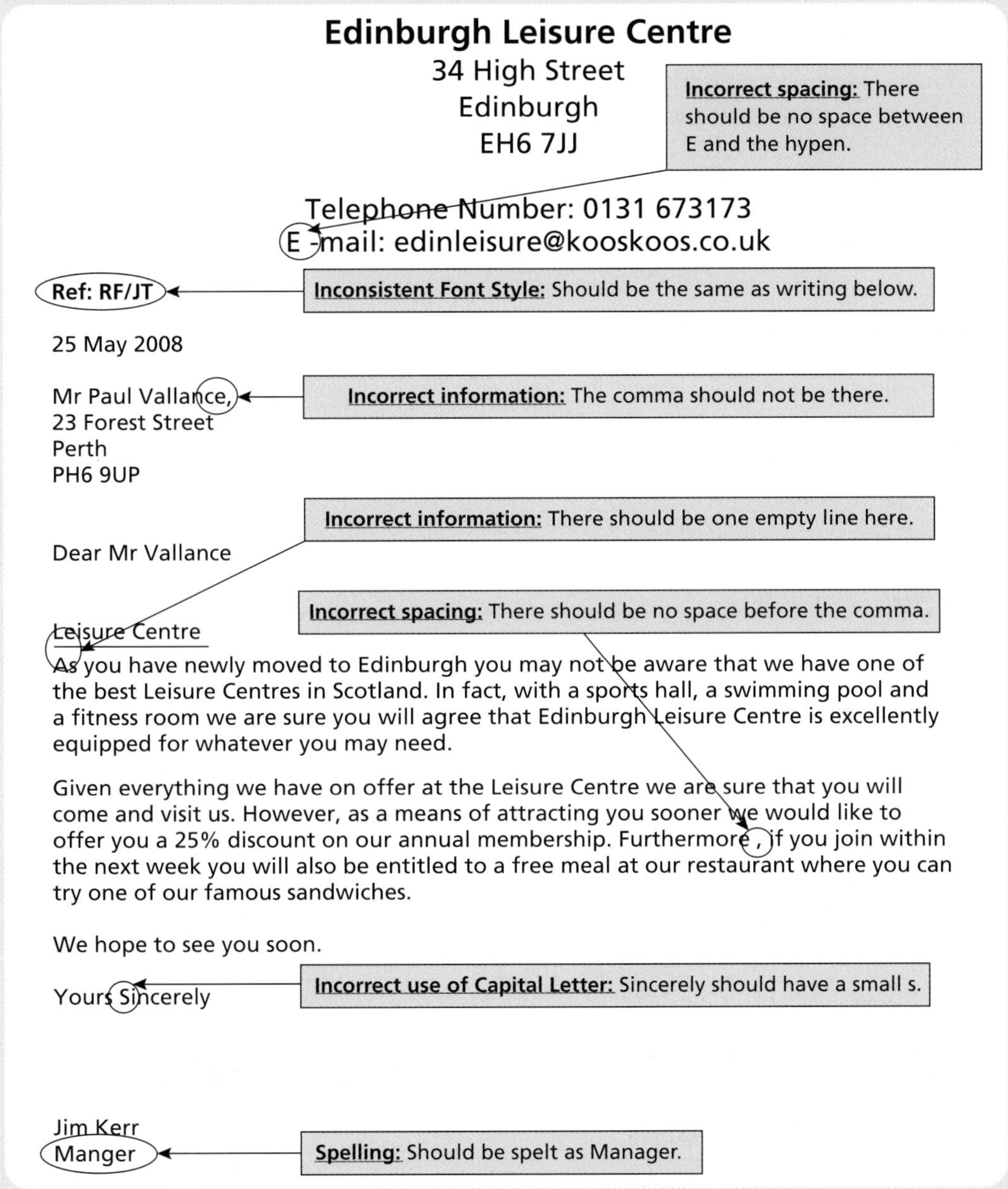

Edinburgh Leisure Centre
34 High Street
Edinburgh
EH6 7JJ

Telephone Number: 0131 673173
E -mail: edinleisure@kooskoos.co.uk

Incorrect spacing: There should be no space between E and the hypen.

Ref: RF/JT

Inconsistent Font Style: Should be the same as writing below.

25 May 2008

Mr Paul Vallance,
23 Forest Street
Perth
PH6 9UP

Incorrect information: The comma should not be there.

Incorrect information: There should be one empty line here.

Dear Mr Vallance

Incorrect spacing: There should be no space before the comma.

Leisure Centre
As you have newly moved to Edinburgh you may not be aware that we have one of the best Leisure Centres in Scotland. In fact, with a sports hall, a swimming pool and a fitness room we are sure you will agree that Edinburgh Leisure Centre is excellently equipped for whatever you may need.

Given everything we have on offer at the Leisure Centre we are sure that you will come and visit us. However, as a means of attracting you sooner we would like to offer you a 25% discount on our annual membership. Furthermore , if you join within the next week you will also be entitled to a free meal at our restaurant where you can try one of our famous sandwiches.

We hope to see you soon.

Yours Sincerely

Incorrect use of Capital Letter: Sincerely should have a small s.

Jim Kerr
Manger

Spelling: Should be spelt as Manager.

Figure 8.2 A business letter

Example continued ➤

PRACTICAL ABILITIES

Example continued

Spreadsheet Example:

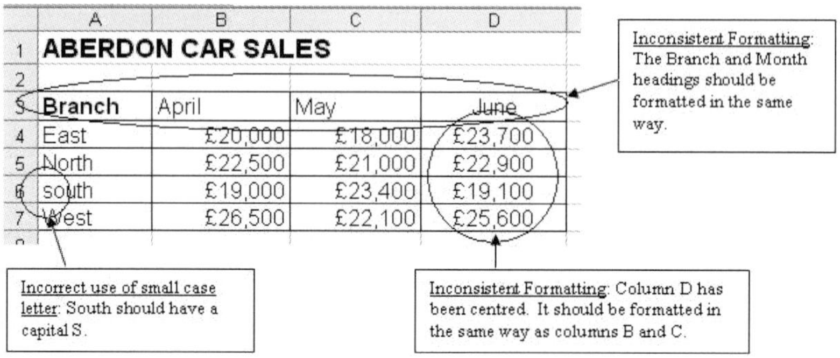

Figure 8.3 An Excel Spreadsheet

Database Example:

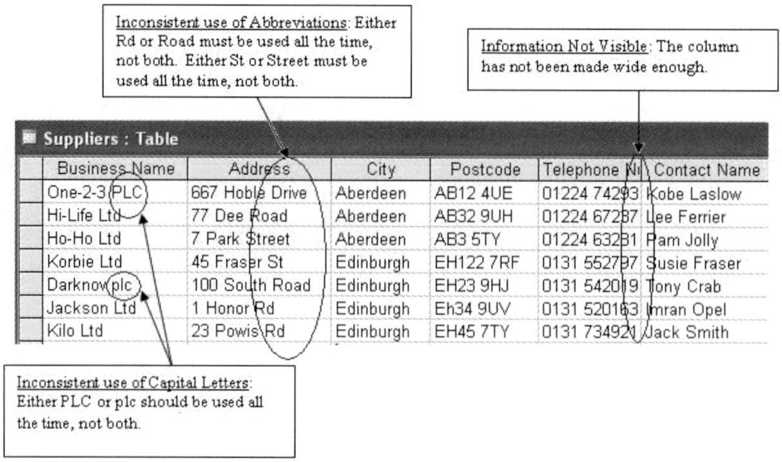

Figure 8.4 An Access Database

Avoiding Keyboarding Errors

As the examples above show, keyboarding errors are easily made. To avoid such problems candidates should thoroughly check every piece of work they complete. It is not enough to think that because a task has been completed that it is correct. All too often keyboarding errors are made without even realising it.

Function Skills

Unlike keyboarding skills which are marked negatively, function skills are marked positively. This means marks are gained for carrying out a task correctly.

How are Function Skills Marks Gained?

Function skills marks are gained by carrying out instructions correctly. At the start of each task, and sometimes within the task itself, there are a number of instructions which tell the candidate how the task should be completed and presented. By carrying out these instructions successfully the candidate can gain function marks.

To understand how function marks are gained it is best to look at an actual example. In the example below the function marks are denoted in brackets as letters e.g. (F). These letters are then displayed against the marked solution to show where the marks were gained. In the actual Practical Abilities project, the function marks will not be displayed like this.

Example

Word Processing Example: Letterhead

A letterhead is needed by the organisation. Display the letterhead effectively (D) using a variety of fonts (F), styles (S), and an appropriate graphic (G). The web address should be included as a footer (Ftr).

Barside Printers
23 Jarvis Road
GLASGOW
G6 7TY

Telephone: 0141 6732829
Email: barprin@jojo.co.uk

The firm's web address is www.barprin.co.uk

Example *continued* ➤

Example continued

Solution (unmarked):

Figure 8.5 A letterhead

Solution (marked):

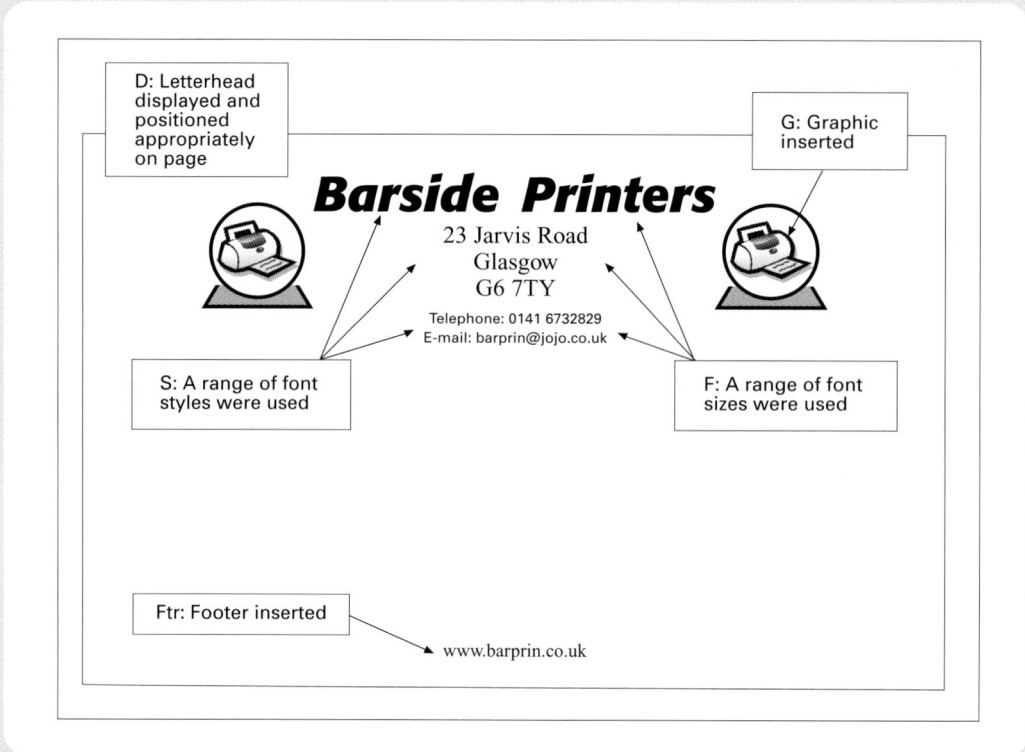

Figure 8.6 The letterhead

Other Problem Areas

Starting a Recall Task

Throughout the Practical Abilities projects a number of tasks involve recalling previous tasks in order to add, delete or amend information. Although most pupils are able to locate earlier tasks they forget to make a copy of the task before starting the new one. This mistake is absolutely crucial and can cost a pupil several marks.

When checking through their project at the end a pupil often finds keyboarding mistakes which require to be corrected. However, if the pupil has not made a copy of their original tasks it will be impossible for them to make the corrections. Worse still, rather than just starting the task again, a pupil may try to correct their final saved copy. The final outcome being that the pupil ends up making more mistakes and losing even more marks. If, however, the pupil had made a copy of their original task, especially the database task, this problem could be avoided.

Missing Printouts

Throughout the Practical Abilities project a number of printouts are requested which are used to mark the project. Unfortunately, a number of pupils forget to print some of their work meaning no marks are gained for some tasks.

The tasks where this tends to be a problem include: i) when a formula view of a spreadsheet is requested, ii) when a specific database printout is requested using a filter or a query, iii) when evidence of sending an email is requested, and iv) when evidence of an internet search is requested.

Labelling Tasks

A number of pupils forget to label their tasks with the task number, their school and their name. This makes the Practical Abilities project very difficult to mark. In some cases, work may not even be marked as it is impossible to decipher which task it is.

Fit for Purpose

A number of tasks, especially in the Credit Project, are assessed as to whether they are fit for purpose or not. Put simply, whether the completed task could be used in a real business situation or not.

The two areas in which this issue is of real importance are: i) when a pupil has to write a letter, memo or email using their own words. If the message the pupil writes makes no sense, reads poorly or is grammatically incorrect marks will be lost, ii) when a pupil is requested to make a form. If the pupil does not leave enough space for details, such as name and address to be entered, marks will be lost. Similarly, if it is not clear on the form where information should be inputted, marks will also be lost.

Manuscript Signs

Manuscript signs are used to provide pupils with keyboarding instructions. Unfortunately many pupils forget to carry out such instructions because they do not know what the signs are asking them to do. Some of the less recognisable manuscript signs and what they mean are shown opposite:

Manuscript Sign	Example	Action that should be taken
(diagonal line through word)	Over the next few year	The word that has been scored out eg "few" should not be typed.
uc	Jarvis hotels	The letter that has been underlined eg "h", should be capitalised eg "H"
stet	Over the next month the following changes	Although the word month has been scored out a dotted line has been placed under it. This means that the word should be used.
in full	info	The word that has been underlined eg info, should be typed in full eg information
NP	. . . .the rest will come back. [Secondly, the people believe in	Where the bracket has been placed indicates where a new paragraph should start.
(caret insertion mark)	Only ^ people turned up (six)	The word in the bracket should be inserted at the point indicated eg only six people turned up
Trs	Ian, Brian,	The words that the trs sign are placed round should be switched eg Brian, Ian,
Run on	There have been some security problems recently. Unfortunately, these do not seem. . . .	The run on sign indicates that a new paragraph should not be taken. Instead, the next sentence should just follow on.
Larger Size	High Street	The word that is underlined should be made bigger eg **High Street**
Justify	Scotland is a terrific place to live and a fantastic country to visit.	The section that is circled should be justified.

Figure 8.7 Proofreading symbols and notes

139

THE STANDARD GRADE ADMINISTRATION EXAM

At the end of the course all candidates sit a written exam which is externally set and marked by the Scottish Qualifications Authority (SQA). The exam covers the whole course and assesses a candidate's Knowledge and Understanding (KU), and Problem Solving (PS) skills. The written exam is worth 60% of a candidate's overall mark (30% KU and 30% PS).

Exam Advice

Every year over a hundred teachers are involved in marking the Standard Grade Administration exam. As part of this process they provide feedback to the SQA on how candidates performed in the exam. Based on this feedback the SQA give advice to teachers and candidates on how exam performance could be improved. The main points are listed below.

Better Knowledge and Understanding is Required

The majority of candidates in the General and Credit papers perform better in PS than KU. It seems many candidates only have basic Knowledge and Understanding of several important terms. This makes it impossible to provide good and detailed answers.

The areas in which Knowledge and Understanding needs to be improved are:

◆ Chapter 1a (Chain of Command; Level of Responsibility; Business Restructuring)

◆ Chapter 1b (Specific roles undertaken by an Administration Assistant in each department; How software applications could be used by each department; Business documents used by each department)

◆ Chapter 2a (Flexible working practices – Homeworking is often confused with teleworking; Carrels; Touchdown areas)

◆ Chapter 2d (The difference between incoming and outgoing mail)

◆ Chapter 3b (The differences between manual and electronic filing; Issues relating to file management)

◆ Chapter 5 (Paper-based sources of information; What an Intranet is – it is often confused with the Internet; E-commerce)

◆ Chapter 6 (Integrated software package; Software applications)

◆ Chapter 7b (Travel guidelines)

Candidates do not read the questions carefully

Even though important words are highlighted many candidates still fail to answer what is being asked. For example, in the question below, the benefits to employees are being asked for. Unfortunately, several candidates will provide the benefits to employers.

Describe **two** benefits to an **employee** of following safe working practices.

Candidates use poor English in their answers

Markers often comment that the level of English used by candidates is disappointing. This makes it difficult for a candidate to provide an answer that makes sense. Punctuation, spelling and grammar are also poor meaning the answers written by candidates are difficult to understand and mark.

It is absolutely vital that all candidates:

◆ Read through their answers at the end to make sure they make sense.

◆ Use punctuation correctly (full stops and commas).

◆ Write neatly and clearly.

Credit level questions requiring justification are answered poorly

In the Credit paper a significant number of questions ask candidates to justify their answers. Unfortunately, few candidates are able to do this satisfactorily.

When asked to justify it is important to *give a reason for the answer* written. For example, in the answer below, the justification has been underlined.

Question

The following problems have been identified.

◆ Sensitive information has been left on computer screens by members of staff when they go for their lunch.

Suggest and justify how the above problem may be overcome. (2 PS – C)

Answer

Use a password protected screensaver. When the screensaver is on no one will be able to see the information until a password is entered.

Other Pieces of Advice

As well as the issues above, a number of other points are worth taking into account:

◆ Answer all the questions. Even if you do not know the answer, give it a go. Marks will not be taken off for getting something wrong.

- ◆ Check how many marks have been allocated to each question. If a question is worth four marks, it means four different points will have to be written to gain full marks.

- ◆ Do not use one word answers. For example, it is not enough to say that a benefit of using email is that it is 'quicker'. Instead, say that it is 'quicker than sending a letter through the post'.

ANSWERS

Chapter 1a: Introduction to Business Organisations: Organisation of Departments

Answer 1

Benefits to an Employee: By making an organisation chart employees will know:

◆ Where they 'fit-into' the organisation e.g. who their manager is, who they are in charge of, what department they work in and who else works there.

◆ How information is passed through the organisation.

◆ How big the organisation is by looking at how many departments and people are on the chart.

Benefits to a Visitor: By making an organisation chart visitors will know:

◆ Which person should be contacted in the organisation to answer a particular query.

◆ Which department the person being visited works in.

◆ Who is in charge of whom.

◆ What different departments are in the organisation and what the organisation does.

◆ How big the organisation is by looking at how many departments and people are on the chart.

Answer 2

Chain of Command: This shows who is in charge of whom and therefore how instructions are passed down an organisation.

Level of Responsibility: This refers to an employee's position within an organisation. The further up the organisation chart an employee is the greater their level of responsibility.

Lateral Relationship: This describes the relationship that employees who are at the same level and within the same department have.

Answer 3

◆ As there are not many levels of management information will move quickly through the organisation.

◆ Decisions should be implemented more quickly as the chain of command is shorter.

◆ Employees at the bottom of the structure are given responsibility and allowed to make decisions which should motivate them.

◆ Such organisations tend to be friendlier as everyone in the organisation knows everyone else.

Answer 4

Recommendation

◆ De-layering

Justification

◆ This will create a flatter structure which will allow information to pass quickly because there will be a shorter chain of command.

◆ In a flat structure staff have to take on more responsibility which should make their jobs more varied.

Answer 5

◆ Loss of jobs ◆ Fewer levels of management ◆ Merger of departments
◆ Employees take on more responsibility ◆ Shorter chain of command
◆ Faster decision making

Chapter 1b: Introduction to Business Organisations: Key Functions of Departments within an Organisation

Answer 1

Suggestion: An email software application

Justification: Allows several job applicants to be contacted at the same time. Email is a very quick way of letting job applicants know they are invited to an interview.

Suggestion: The internet

Justification: Job adverts placed on the internet would be seen by lots of people.

Suggestion: The intranet

Justification: All staff can access internal job adverts or new updated health and safety procedures easily from a networked computer.

Suggestion: A telephone

Justification: It is a quick way of contacting a successful job applicant to let them know they've got the job.

Answer 2

◆ Wages could be calculated using formulae – fewer mistakes would be made.

◆ Cells on the sheet can be formatted to make certain information stand out.

◆ Charts can be created from the financial information on the spreadsheet.

Answer 3

◆ A more efficient service can be provided by a specialist Administration Department.

◆ Noisy equipment such as photocopiers no longer required to be located in individual departments.

◆ Basic and boring tasks such as filing and franking mail will not be overlooked.

◆ More space will be available in other departments if staff are moved to an Administration Department.

◆ It will be easier and more cost effective to introduce new equipment such as scanners.

Answer 4

Purchases Department Administration Assistant

◆ Completing purchase orders.

◆ Contacts suppliers to request a catalogue of prices.

◆ Filing supplier catalogues.

◆ Maintaining a database of all suppliers' names and addresses.

Human Resources Manager

◆ Interviewing staff for the department.

◆ Motivating staff that work in the department.

◆ Managing the Human Resources budget.

◆ Giving advice to other departments on human resource legislation.

Wages Clerk

◆ Calculating wages.

◆ Paying wages electronically.

◆ Counting out money to go into wage packets.

◆ Preparing wage slips.

Office Manager

- Supervising and motivating administration staff.
- Liaising with other departments to find out what work needs to be done.
- Interviewing staff for the department.
- Checking completed work for quality

Chapter 2a: The Working Environment: Office Layout

Answer 1

- As everybody is working in the same area it can get rather noisy meaning it is difficult for employees to concentrate.
- It is difficult to have a meeting in private because there may not be any rooms available.
- Noisy equipment can distract employees.
- Visitors or staff can move about the office without restriction. This means they may come across something that is confidential and which they are not meant to see.
- The lighting, heating and ventilation will be the same throughout the office. This may not suit certain departments or employees.

Answer 2

Telephone: Allows you to obtain an instant response from the employee.

Voicemail: If the employee is not available a message can be left for the employee to contact the office.

Fax: Paper-based documents that would normally have to be posted can be sent within a few seconds down a telephone line.

Email: Messages and attached files can be sent to the employee very quickly meaning there are no delays. The employee can reply to the message within a few minutes.

Answer 3

Hot Room: Provides homeworkers with somewhere to interview customers or talk to clients in private. Taking a client to a private room is a lot more professional than asking them to a house for a meeting. The meeting that takes place may be confidential.

Carrels: Provides a homeworker with privacy so they can get on with their work. Can be booked in advance so a homeworker will not make a wasted trip. The carrel will have facilities which the homeworker may not have access to at home.

Answer 4

Job Sharing: A job share could be offered to experienced employees who intend to leave. This means they will not have to work full time.

Hot desks: The organisation should create hot desks which homeworkers could book before coming into the office.

Email or Telephone: Procedures should be put into place whereby all homeworkers are contacted by telephone or email about any upcoming meetings.

Chapter 2b: The Working Environment: Safe Working Practices

Answer 1

- Make sure a sign is placed on the fire door stating that the door must never be locked and the area must always be kept free and clear. All employees should also be made aware of this.
- Advise employees to always switch equipment off at the socket before opening it. Basic safety training should cover this issue.
- The telephone could be moved closer to telephone sockets so that wires do not have to trail across the floor. If this is not possible, the wire should be placed in a cable tidy which is then highlighted with hazard tape so that it can be easily seen.
- Advise employees to never place liquids on top of electrical equipment. Basic safety training should cover this issue.

Answer 2

- Provide employees with adjustable chairs, wrist-rests and footrests so that repetitive strain injury is avoided.
- Give employees regular rest breaks to ensure aches, pains and eyestrain are avoided.
- Provide glare guards or put blinds across all windows so that the Sun does not glare against computer screens and cause eye strain.
- Provide regular eye tests to check an employee's eyesight.
- Provide employees with training on how to adjust their chair, screen and other equipment they may use.

Answer 3

Action: Switch the photocopier off.

Justification: The photocopier is already smoking. By switching it off the problem should not get any worse.

Action: Do not try to open the photocopier.

Justification: By opening the photocopier an employee could put themselves in danger. The smoke may be an indication of a small fire inside the photocopier.

Action: Inform those in the area that the photocopier is smoking and should not be used.

Justification: This is so no one else puts themselves in danger.

Action: Attach an 'Out of Order' or 'Do Not Use' sign to the photocopier.

Justification: This is so no one else comes into the room and tries to use the equipment.

Action: Complete a Hazard Report Form immediately and pass to your line manager.

Justification: This problem needs to be dealt with immediately. All health and safety problems should be recorded. The line manager should have the experience to deal with the problem effectively.

Answer 4

- They could carry out their duties in a safe manner and without putting other employees in danger.
- They should follow the health and safety procedures of the organisation.
- They should use any health and safety equipment or protective clothing as they have been trained to do so.
- They should work with the employer to ensure good health and safety in the workplace.

Answer 5

- They must ensure entrances and exits to the workplace are safe.
- They must ensure equipment is safe and properly maintained.
- They must ensure regular health and safety checks are undertaken to ensure a safe working environment.
- They must ensure protective clothing is provided where necessary.
- They must ensure dangerous substances are properly stored and used according to instructions.
- They must ensure employees are given adequate health and safety training so that they can carry out their duties safely.
- They must ensure the organisation has a health and safety policy that all employees are made aware of.

Chapter 2c: The Working Environment: Reception Services

Answer 1

Action: Have a list or catalogue of products with prices in one of his drawers.

Reason: The receptionist will be able to answer the query. The receptionist will look very professional and organised. The level of customer service will be improved.

Action: Request that an organisation chart and photographs of key personnel be displayed in the reception area.

Reason: The receptionist will be able to refer to the chart and photographs when answering the query. The receptionist will look professional and well organised.

Answer 2

Quality: Polite and friendly to visitors

Justification: So visitors feel welcomed when they visit the organisation.

Quality: Good ICT skills

Justification: The receptionist will be responsible for undertaking a number of administrative tasks that will require the use of ICT.

Quality: Tidy and well organised

Justification: If a receptionist's desk looks untidy it will provide a negative image of the organisation. If the receptionist is disorganised she may not be able to complete all her work on time.

Answer 3

◆ Appointments cannot be double booked.

◆ Appointments can be amended or deleted very easily.

◆ Reminders of appointment can be set up.

◆ If a meeting happens at a regular time every week a diary entry can be set up to show this.

◆ Additional details can be added to an entry. For example, details of important papers which need to be taken to a particular meeting.

Answer 4

◆ Make sure all employees make an entry in the Staff Signing In book when they arrive for work. Should they leave during the day, the Staff In/Out book should be completed.

◆ All visitors should make an entry in the Visitors' Book when they arrive for a meeting with a manager.

Answer 5

◆ Create a waiting area where visitors can sit and help themselves to tea/coffee.

◆ Make sure all doors off the reception area are locked or require swipe card entry. Visitors should be collected from reception or taken by the receptionist to the manager's office.

◆ Issue all homeworkers with ID badges. Advise them that these must be worn and displayed when they come into work.

Answer 6

Method: Lock all doors that come off the reception area.

Justification: Visitors will be unable to walk directly through to the main office.

Method: Check employees' ID badges

Justification: This will stop those without authority just walking into the main office unchallenged.

Method: Man the reception area

Justification: This will act as a visual deterrent to those wanting to cause trouble.

Method: Employ a security guard

Justification: This will act as a visual deterrent to those wanting to cause trouble.

Answer 7

Aggressive visitor: Use a soft voice to try and calm the visitor. If they refuse, call security. No attempts should be made to restrain the visitor.

Reason: Using a soft voice will not antagonise the visitor and is more likely to calm them down. Security guards are trained to deal with difficult situations. Under no circumstances should the receptionist put herself in danger.

Ill Receptionist: Someone else who has been trained should man the reception area.

Reason: A reception area without a receptionist gives out a negative and unprofessional image of an organisation.

Chapter 2d: The Working Environment: Mail Handling

Answer 1

◆ Sign for Special Deliveries and parcels.

◆ Accept the mail in the morning from the Postman.

◆ Take the mail to the Mail Room.

Answer 2

◆ Mail Room staff should start work an hour earlier.

◆ Once mail has been opened and sorted it should be taken directly to employees without delay.

Answer 3

◆ Mail that is sent out with an organisation.

◆ Mail sent between the organisation and another party e.g. customer or business.

Answer 4

A Letter Opener: Shaped like a knife, but with a narrower blade, a letter opener is used to open an envelope quickly and neatly without damaging the contents within.

Date Stamp: A date stamp is used to stamp items of mail with the date on which they are received by an organisation. Shaped like a hammer head, a date stamp usually has revolving rubber cogs on its face which can be changed according to the date on which the stamp is used.

Stapler: A stapler is used to attach enclosures to a covering letter so that items do not get lost or detached from each other as the mail is being dealt with.

Photocopier: A photocopier is used to make exact copies of correspondence that are to be seen by more than one person in the organisation.

Scanner: A scanner is a device that converts paper based documents into electronic form. It works to some extent in a similar fashion to a photocopier.

Answer 4

◆ Advise staff of the time at which mail is taken to the Post Office or collect items of mail from departments at a set time which all staff are made aware of.

◆ Weigh and check the size of mail before franking it.

Answer 5

Big and Small Letter Measure: This device judges whether an item of mail should be priced as a big or a small letter. Basically a plastic board with two rectangular holes cut into it; a big and small letter measure shows the maximum size that a big or small letter can be.

Scales: Scales are used to weigh mail. Once an item has been weighed its postage cost can be calculated by looking in a Royal Mail pricing booklet. Some electronic scales are able to price mail automatically as the postage costs of differently weighted items have been programmed into the scales. More sophisticated machines are even able to price items which are being sent Special Delivery or overseas.

Franking Machine: A franking machine is used by a Mail Room instead of stamps. Using a dial or a keypad located on the machine, the operator sets the price at which each item of mail will be franked. Each item of mail is then fed through the machine which franks the envelope with the postal charge.

Answer 6

Method: Intranet

Justification: All staff have access to the intranet via the organisation's network and can easily check what vacancies are available.

Method: Second Class Letter

Justification: The information does not have to be there very quickly. Inviting someone to an interview should be done formally using a letter.

Method: Memo

Justification: Sending a memo shows that the message is important and will provide a permanent record of the new procedure.

Method: Email or Fax

Justification: Both these methods will get the message there within 20 minutes as it is sent down a telephone line. Both will also send a copy of the actual document, unlike a telephone call.

Answer 7

1st Class: Cheap and the item will get there quickly i.e. within 2 days.

2nd Class: Very cheap and the item will get there within 3 days.

Special Delivery: The item has guaranteed delivery and needs to be signed for which provides proof of delivery.

Courier: Can offer same day delivery for very important items. The item must be signed for which provides proof of delivery.

Chapter 3a: Storage and Retrieval of Information: Purpose of Filing

Answer 1

Shredder: This will destroy out-of-date documents and prevent them getting into the hands of criminals after disposal.

Use of 'Out Guides' or 'Absent Markers': These let employees know that a file is currently in use by another employee.

Only documents stamped with 'file' should be filed: Documents not 'file' stamped can be destroyed – files will not be cluttered with irrelevant information.

Chapter 3b: Storage and Retrieval of Information: Methods

Answer 1

Method: Alphabetical

Justification:
◆ An alphabetical filing system is easy to use and understand. As long as you know the alphabet and the name of the customer you are looking for, it is fairly straightforward to locate and file documents.
◆ Such a filing system is also easy to set up as all you need is knowledge of the alphabet and enough filing cabinets to put the files in.
◆ As the system is so easy to use and set up it is popular with small- to medium-sized organisations that do not have too many customers.

Method: Numerical

Justification:
◆ Useful when the organisation has lots of customers who have the same surname. As long as the customer remembers their file number, the problem of finding a customer's file when they have the same surname as other customers is eliminated.
◆ As files are in number order it is fairly easy to understand the system and thus file files correctly.
◆ Unlike an alphabetical system, a numerical system can be easily expanded without a massive reorganisation of the existing files. New files are just added to the end of the current files, rather than throughout, as is the case with an alphabetical system.

Answer 2
◆ Scan documents into digital form and then save onto a computer.
◆ Record the documents onto microfiche which can then be viewed on a reader.

Answer 3
◆ Files are saved using appropriate file names.
◆ Associated files are placed in appropriate folders.
◆ Obsolete files are deleted regularly.

Answer 4
◆ Create folders and sub folders into which each department can place their files.
◆ Burn or download the database file onto a CD, or a USB flash drive

Chapter 3c: Storage and Retrieval of Information: Security of Information

Answer 1

Suggestion: Use passwords or computer swipe cards.

Justification: Without the password or a computer swipe card an employee will not be able to access the confidential files.

Suggestion: Use a password protected screensaver.

Justification: Information on the screen will not be visible and a password needs to be inputted before the information can be viewed again.

Suggestion: Install anti-virus software.

Justification: The software deletes suspicious emails and eliminates viruses already on the system.

Answer 2

Provisions

- That the information is collected and processed lawfully.
- That the organisation only collects and holds information that it is authorised by the Data Protection Registrar to do so.
- That information collected is only used in a way that has been authorised by the Data Protection Registrar.
- That information is only provided to other organisations if authorised by the Data Protection Registrar.
- That information collected is accurate and kept up to date.
- That only information needed by the organisation is collected. It should not be excessive or irrelevant.
- That information is held securely.
- That information is held for only as long as it is needed.

Answer 3

- Backing up involves taking an exact copy of a document so that if the original is lost or destroyed there is a copy to replace it.

Answer 4

- If a system crashes information will not be permanently lost.
- To protect against viruses destroying information.
- To save time having to collect information again.

Chapter 4: Reprographics

Answer 1

Laminator: A laminator is a piece of equipment which coats paper or card in a thin film of clear plastic. By coating the document in a protective plastic coating it becomes a lot more durable. Laminators are used to protect health and safety or fire notices which are placed around a building.

Binder: A binder is a piece of equipment which allows a multi-page document to be fastened together using a plastic binder. By binding a document together it is less likely that pages will come loose and be lost. Documents that tend to be bound include reports, manuals or instruction booklets.

Scanner: A scanner is an electronic device which uses a light-sensitive scanning device to convert paper-based documents into a digital form. Once converted, the documents can then be saved as computer files. Organisations can use scanners to scan all incoming mail.

Hole Punch: A hole punch is a piece of equipment which makes holes in a paper document so that it can be placed in a ring binder.

Staple Gun: Some reprographics departments have powerful staple guns which can staple multi-page documents which a traditional stapler could not.

Desk Top Publishing (DTP) Software: This software allows a reprographics assistant to bring together text, graphics and photographs in one document ready for publishing. Magazines, booklets, newsletters, catalogues, posters and other such documents may be produced in this way.

Answer 2

Suggestion: Stapler

Advantage: A stapler fastens pages together meaning they will not come loose.

Suggestion: Laminator

Advantage: Laminating protects a poster from dirt, water, wear and tear by coating the document in a film of plastic.

Suggestion: Hole Punch

Advantage: By punching holes in each new page they can be easily added to the ring binder meaning they will not fall out, come loose or get lost.

Answer 3

Suggestion: Introduce a photocopying request form.

Justification: The instructions on the form help to carry out the photocopying correctly. The form will detail exactly how the photocopying is to be completed.

Suggestion: Use a qualified engineer to repair electrical equipment.

Justification: By trying to repair the photocopier the employee is putting their health and safety in danger.

Answer 4

◆ An outside agency has better equipment and specialist staff which means the photocopying will be done to a higher quality.

◆ An outside agency may be able to produce colour copies on glossy paper which cannot be done in-house.

◆ An outside agency will have an industrial photocopier which is able to produce thousands of copies very quickly.

Answer 5

Recommendation: In-House

Reasons:

◆ Only black and white copying required.

◆ Will be cheaper than outside agency.

◆ No special requirements e.g. the letters do not need to be copied onto glossy paper.

◆ An In-House photocopier will be able to handle 200 copies.

Chapter 5: Sources of Information

Answer 1

◆ Software applications such as Word, Excel, Access and PowerPoint can be shared by all employees as they are accessed through the organisation's server.

◆ By sharing information over an intranet an organisation no longer needs to issue paper memos to every employee which will cut costs.

◆ Employees will find it easier to find information on an intranet as most have a search facility similar to those on the internet.

◆ Discussion forums, just like those on the internet, can be set up for employees to exchange ideas and discuss work-related issues. This should improve work flow.

◆ Employees can access information on the intranet from any networked computer.

◆ New information can be added very quickly meaning employees are always aware of what is happening in the organisation.

Answer 2

◆ Access to more customers. An organisation located in Scotland can sell products all over the world.

◆ Lower costs. An online retailer does not need to spend money on lots of shops or employees to sell their products.

◆ Products can be sold 24 hours a day, 7 days a week. Unlike many shops which close at night, an internet site is open all the time.

Answer 3

Hyperlink: A hot spot on an internet site that provides direct access to another page or site.

Search Engine: A facility which helps a user locate information on the internet. It works by matching the keywords the user has typed into the search engine against those in the search engine's database of internet sites.

Answer 4

Information: A site should contain information that is useful, honest and correct. The writing on a site should use a font style and font size that is readable.

Hyperlinks: There should be hyperlinks which provide direct access to other pages on the site or to another web site. This makes a site more user friendly as information that is linked can be directly connected even though it is on two separate pages.

Search Engine facility: Finding information on a website can be very difficult. By putting a search engine facility on their home page, an organisation makes it easier for users to find the information they want from the site quickly and efficiently.

E-commerce facility: In order to take advantage of those customers who wish to purchase online an organisation must offer an e-commerce facility on its site.

Answer 5

◆ Undertake market research of customers and other businesses by researching their websites or by setting up surveys for them to complete online.

◆ To advertise products on the organisation's website by showing pictures of them.

◆ Sell products on the organisation's website via an e-commerce facility.

Chapter 6: Preparation and Presentation of Information

Answer 1

◆ All documents sent by the organisation are the same and hence look very professional.

◆ Staff can be easily trained to use a standard house style.

◆ Staff will become very familiar with the standard house style meaning fewer mistakes and errors will be made.

◆ Checking work will be easier as all documents are produced using an identical layout.

Answer 2

A Flipchart Pad: Is useful as keywords can be written on the pad which act as a permanent record of what was said.

An OHP: Is useful as it allows information held on A4 acetates to be displayed on a big screen for everyone to see.

A Projector: Is useful as it allows information held on a computer screen to be displayed on a big screen for everyone to see.

An Interactive Whiteboard: Is useful as the presenter can interact with the board in order to bring up different pieces of information e.g. a chart from a spreadsheet, a memo from the sales director.

Answer 3

◆ Printer ◆ Scanner ◆ Laminator

Answer 4

◆ The purchase of an integrated software package is often cheaper than buying software applications individually.

◆ Information can be easily transferred and linked between applications within the package. For example, Microsoft allows information from an Access database to be merged with a word processed letter in Word.

◆ Each application in the package is designed in a similar way. This makes it easier for employees to learn how to use each application. For example, in each application of Microsoft, the instruction to 'Print' is found in the File menu.

◆ Different applications in the package can be open at the same time.

Answer 5

Spreadsheet software e.g. Excel: A spreadsheet will allow him to display statistical information in a chart which is easier to understand.

Presentation software e.g. PowerPoint: A presentation package will allow him to create presentations that include charts, colourful backgrounds and special effects. These presentations can then be shown on a big screen using a projector which would make them easier to read.

Answer 6

◆ Details can be amended and edited easily.

◆ Details from the database can be merged with a word processed document.

◆ Records can be searched for using the search facility.

◆ Records can be put in order e.g. alphabetical, using the sort facility.

Answer 7

◆ Mail merge the customer database with the letter. By doing this the letter will only have to be typed once.

◆ Use a spreadsheet and formulae to do the calculations. As long as the formulae are done correctly the profit figure calculated will be correct.

◆ Use a desk top publishing package such as Publisher which has a number of templates which allow professional looking adverts to be created easily and quickly using different formatting techniques.

Answer 8

◆ Currency ◆ Text ◆ Date ◆ Percentage

Answer 9

◆ An email message can be prepared and sent very quickly at virtually no cost.

◆ Messages can be prepared and sent with a flag that indicates how important the message is.

◆ Messages can be prepared with a tracking option which lets the user know when their message has been received and read.

◆ A user can set up their inbox to display their email messages in a number of different ways. For example, in date received order or in alphabetical order.

◆ Information held in the calendar, task, contacts and notes functions can be easily updated and altered without making a mess.

◆ Messages can be sent with attachments.

Answer 10

◆ The figures are easier to compare if in a line graph.

◆ It is easier to identify trends in the figures if displayed in a line graph.

◆ A line graph is easier to understand than a table of sales figures.

Answer 11

◆ In a word processed table with headings and a title.

◆ In a spreadsheet chart which is clearly labelled.

Answer 12

Recommendation: The Name field should be split up into First Name and Surname.

Justification: This will allow an alphabetical sort to take place on the Surname field.

Answer 13

◆ Date

Chapter 7a: Travel Arrangements

Answer 1

◆ AA/RAC handbooks would provide independent advice on hotels. It is more likely that a suitable hotel with the facilities required for the business trip will be booked if an AA/RAC handbook is used.

◆ Timetables provide accurate information on departure and arrival times of buses and trains. By using a timetable it will be easier to prepare an accurate itinerary.

Answer 2

Advice: Find out what time John Barr needs to arrive in Rome.

Justification: If John needs to get there in the morning an early flight will have to be booked.

Advice: Find out where in Rome the exhibition is.

Justification: This will make it easier to select an appropriate hotel close to the exhibition.

Advice: Ask John to complete a travel/accommodation request form.

Justification: This will provide Jerry with the information he needs to complete the task successfully.

Advice: Find out if he has any special requirements.

Justification: If John is disabled, the airline and hotel will have to be made aware so that appropriate arrangements can be made.

Advice: Find out what the budget for the trip is.

Justification: If there is not a lot of money a cheap hotel may have to be chosen.

Answer 3

Suggestion: Visa

Justification: When travelling to some countries a visa is required for entry. Without a valid visa an employee will be unable to pass through customs points and will be sent home.

Suggestion: European Health Insurance Card (EHIC).

Justification: This card is important as it entitles the employee to free emergency medical treatment in all European Union countries.

Suggestion: Travel Insurance Documentation.

Justification: This documentation is important as it can be used to obtain health care and legal assistance while abroad. Travel insurance is of particular use while travelling in non-European Union countries.

Suggestion: Driving License.

Justification: A full UK driving license will be needed if the employee intends to hire a car while abroad.

Chapter 7b: Travel: Paying for Business Trips

Answer 1

◆ Personal Cheque   ◆ Cash   ◆ Debit Card   ◆ Travellers' Cheques

Answer 2

- The employee will not have to carry large amounts of cash which is safer.
- They are very secure. A pin number or a security code on the back of the card is required before a payment is authorised.
- Expenses are easy to track because a bill is sent to the organisation at the end of each month.
- They can be used abroad.

Answer 3

EXPENSE CLAIM FORM		
All receipts and invoices should be attached where available		

Name: *Tommy Bell*	Department: *Sales and Marketing*		

Date: *26/8/08 – 28/8/08*		Total Expenditure	
TRAVEL (please detail)		£	pp
EASYAIR Flight (Glasgow to London return)		125	00
ACCOMMODATION (please detail) Dorset Hotel – 2 nights Bed and Breakfast		150	00
MEALS (please detail) Dinner × 2 (£15 + £15)		30	00
OTHER EXPENSES (please detail) Taxi (£5 + £5.50) Drinks – Bar Bill at Hotel (£5 + £10)		10 15	50 00
TOTAL EXPENSES DUE		330	50
Employee's Signature: *Tommy Bell*		Date: *2/10/08*	